WISE OWL Polysyllables:

Word Identification Strategies of English:

Orthographic Word Logic

Advanced Reading Skills
for Young Readers

Copyright © 2015 DONALD L. POTTER

All rights reserved.

ISBN-10: 151503822X
ISBN-13: 978-1515038221

Cover Picture by Daniel González

www.donpotter.net

DEDICATION

TO MR. FRANK ROGERS

OF TACOMA, WASHINGTON

CREATOR OF THE TATRAS

(**T**EACHING **A**MERICA **T**O **R**EAD AND SPELL)

VERTICAL PHONICS READING PROGRAM

The Wise Old Owl

A wise old owl lived in an oak.
The more he saw the less he spoke.
The less he spoke the more he heard.
Why can't we all be like that wise old bird?

Submitted by Daniel González,
an eight-year-old *Wise Owl Polysyllables'* student
in Australia.

71 WISE OWL Phonograms for Decoding Polysyllabic Words

Advanced Reading Skills for Advancing Readers

Teaching Sequence

Phonogram Group A: 137 Words

a o s m d h b th e ee u
t n r w er f i y l c

Phonogram Group B: 184 Words

or v p wh

Phonogram Group C: 147 Words

ar (a r) ng sh ay ai igh k ck
ur ir wor j ew ould gn x

Phonogram Group D: 218 Words

z aw au kn wr oi oy
ph oa ui dge tion

Phonogram Group E: 250 Words

g ou ow ch ea oo ey ei
…ed augh ough pn

Group A Symbol-to-Sound Relationships

a o s m d h b th e ee u t n r w er f i y l c

Only words with these letters and letter combinations will be used in Group A. A single dot over the vowels à and ò indicates the schwa sound (short ŭ). The *American Heritage Dictionary* is the authority for word pronunciations, accents, and syllable divisions. In this program, each Group uses only the new phonograms for that Group and phonograms from the previously taught Groups.

Group A1: Wise Owl Polysyllables

A1-1. in-**stall**-ment: My dad is buying a car on the **installment** plan. He is *making payments* every month *until he has paid for it*.

A1-2. **set**-tle-ment: When the settlers came to America, they built *villages to live* in called **settlements**. Did you see the word *set* in settlement?

A1-3. **dem**-òn-strate: My cooking teacher was able to **demonstrate** how to bake a delicious apple pie. She *showed us how* to make one right there in the classroom. It was a great demonstration. The pie was delicious!

A1-4. re-**sent**-ment: Henry felt a lot of **resentment** when his best friend told him that he was not good enough to be on the track team. He *felt hurt* and was *upset* with his friend.

A1-5. de-**test**-à-ble: The new movie was **detestable**. Everybody *disliked it a lot*. They said it was so bad that they did not want to watch it again.

A1-6. ad-**min**-is-ter: The nice nurse had to **administer** the bitter medicine to the sick child. The nurse added a little sugar to make it taste better. To **administer** is *to give*.

A1-7. **bit**-ter-ness: Jill felt a lot of **bitterness** when she was not invited to Terry's birthday party. She was *very unhappy*. **Bitterness** is a *sharp taste* in your mouth *without sweetness*, like a lemon without sugar.

A1-8. de-**ter**-mined: Mr. Potter is **determined** to teach everybody to read well. *He has made up his mind not to let anyone stop him* from teaching everyone to read well. His <u>WISE OWL Polysyllables</u> program will help you read much better.

A1-9. in-ter-**me**-di-ate: Judy is an **intermediate** swimmer. She is neither a beginning nor an advanced swimmer. Her skills are *somewhere in between*.

A1-10. **in**-ter-state: We took the **interstate** highways all the way from Texas to Michigan. **Inter** means *between* so **interstate** means *between states*.

A1-11. ob-**lit**-er-ate: The wrecking crew smashed a huge weight suspended from a crane into the old apartment building. They were able to **obliterate** the building by hitting it again and again until it was *completely destroyed*.

A1-12. **wil**-der-ness: We like to camp out in the **wilderness** under the starry sky. Not very many people live in the **wilderness**. It is an *uninhabited and uncultivated area* like a big woods without any houses or cultivated fields.

A1-13. sen-ti-**men**-tàl: Sometimes I feel **sentimental** about my boyhood home in Indiana. I *miss* the glittering white snow in the winter and the luscious green grass in the summer. I *feel sad* when I think of all my family that lives so far away.

A1-14. **lone**-li-ness: I think everyone feels **loneliness** from time to time. **Loneliness** is the *sadness that comes from not having friends*. I hope you have lots of good friends and never feel lonely.

A1-15. re-**lent**-less: Mr. Potter is **relentless** in his pursuit to teach all children how to read well. He *never gives up*, no matter what! He is typing these sentences so YOU can read better.

A1-16. **rest**-less-ness: Nate gets to feeling lots of **restlessness** in school when spring is just around the corner. He is *unable to rest* because he wants to go outside and play.

A1-17. in-**hab**-i-tànt: Many wonderful people inhabit the South Sea Islands. They are inhabitants of the luscious green islands. An **inhabitant** is *a person who lives or occupies a place*.

A1-18. as-**tron**-ȯ-mer: In 1929 the **astronomer** Edward Hubble discovered that galaxies are receding (moving away) from each other. **Astronomers** are *scientists who use powerful telescopes to study the universe.*

A1-19. de-**lib**-er-ȧte: It is important to make a **deliberate** choice about what college you are going to attend. Take your time, consider all the facts, and then make your decision. It should be *done consciously and intentionally.*

A1-20. il-**lit**-er-ȧte: An **illiterate** person is a *person who cannot read.* Mr. Potter works hard to teach everyone how to read well so no one will be **illiterate**.

A1-21. in-ter-**mit**-tent: The light in the living room has an **intermittent** short circuit. It keeps going *off and on at irregular intervals.* We need to fix the short circuit so the light will not keep going on and off.

A1-22. **ten**-der-ness: A mother bear is tender with her little cubs. She is *gentle and kind* with them. They experience a lot of **tenderness** from their loving mother.

A1-23. in-**tol**-er-ȧ-ble: John quit his job at the big factory. He said the noise was **intolerable**. It was so loud that he was *unable to endure* it another day.

A1-24. con-**si**-der-ȧte: John was **considerate** to the new boy at school. He got to know the new boy and helped him make friends and learn all the rules. He was *concerned and caring* about his wellbeing.

GROUP A2: Wise Owl Polysyllables

A2-1. nin*e*-**teen**th: Jim was the **nineteenth** boy in line. He was number 19. There were eighteen in front of him.

A2-2. ther-**mom**-e-ter: A **thermometer** *measures heat*. You can use a **thermometer** to check your temperature if you feel sick. You might have a high fever and be contagious to others.

A2-3. dis-**trib**-ute: Our teacher asked Marge to **distribute** the papers. She asked her to *pass them out* to the students.

A2-4. en-**thu**-si-as-m: Mr. Potter has a lot of **enthusiasm** for teaching kids to read better. He is *really excited* about it. He makes learning to read lots of fun for his students.

A2-5. il-**lu**-mi-nate: A bright light can **illuminate** a room so we can see to read a good book. It *lights up* the room.

A2-6: **il**-lus-trate: Tim decided to **illustrate** his story with lots of good pictures. To **illustrate** means *to use pictures to help people understand the story better*.

A2-7: in-**dus**-tri-al: An **industrial** grade drill will drill a hole through the hardest metal. It is for heavy-duty **industrial** use.

A2-8. in-**nu**-mer-à-ble: Jim has **innumerable** baseball cards. He has so many baseball cards that he *can't count them all*. Innumerable refers to a number *too big to count*.

A2-9. **in**-stru-ment: A guitar is a great musical **instrument**. Mr. Potter plays a Gibson ES-125 guitar. It is a beautiful arch top electric guitar that he bought in 1966.

A2-10. mis-un-der-**stand**: Did you **misunderstand** the question? Yes, I *fail to understand* it. Please ask me again.

A2-11. mon-u-**men**-tal: June made a **monumental** decision when she decided to become a nurse. It was a *major, life changing decision*.

A2-12. **sub**-sti-tute: We had a **substitute** teacher yesterday when our regular teacher was absent. He was really cool because he told exciting adventure stories.

A2-13. un-der-**stand**-a-ble: Brayden was very **understandable** for a two year old. It was *easy to understand* what he said.

A2-14. de-**fense**-less: Jane took the poor, **defenseless** kitten to her house to live. The kitten *could not defend* or *take care* of itself. The fluffy little kitten is safe now in Jane's nice house.

A2-15. dis-**taste**-ful: The ice tea was very **distasteful**. It *tasted terrible* because it was made with city water.

A2-16. ful-**fill**-ment: Becoming a Classical Guitarist was the **fulfillment** of John's boyhood dream. He can play the beautiful Bach "Chaconne" just like Andres Segovia.

A2-17. fun-dà-**men**-tal: Reading is a **fundamental** skill. It is a *basic* skill that we need to be successful in school. Every subject requires the ability to read.

A2-18. in-de-**fen**-si-ble: The castle was **indefensible** because the walls were not high enough or thick enough to stop the enemy soldiers from climbing over the walls. The soldiers in the castle *could not defend* it.

A2-19. in-**def**-i-nite: The principal said that Harry's suspension from school was **indefinite.** He was *not sure how long* it would be before Harry could go back to school.

A2-20. in-**dif**-fer-ent: Joan was **indifferent** as to how long it would take her to hike up the hill. She *didn't really care* how long it would take.

A2-21. in-**fal**-li-ble: **Infallible** means *incapable of making a mistake*. I have never met anybody that is **infallible**. Have you?

A2-22. ref-er-**en**-dum: The people had to vote on a **referendum** to see if the citizens were willing to pay for the new school that the School Board wanted to build.

A2-23. re-**fine**-ment: A **refinement** is *a small improvement*. Sometimes **refinement** can make a big difference. A **refinement** in your pencil grip can make a big difference in how well you are able to write.

A2-24. re-dis-**tri**-bute: The teacher took up the candy she had distributed to the class and **redistributed** it to make sure everybody got an equal amount. She *passed it out again*.

Group A3: Wise Owl Polysyllables

A3-1. **use**-ful-ness: **Usefulness** is the *quality or fact of being useful*. The **usefulness** of a pencil lies in its ability to put letters and designs on paper.

A3-2. ab-so-**lute**-ly: Are you **absolutely** sure you know what **absolutely** means? **Absolutely**! Words ending in -ly are adverbs. Add -ly to absolute and you get **absolutely**. **Absolutely** means *with no qualification, restriction, or limitation.*

A3-3. **al**-ter-nàte-ly: When you do things by *taking turns,* you do them **alternately**. Alexis and Ayden read **alternately**. They *take turns.*

A3-4. **brill**-iant-ly: The great Andres Segovia played the guitar **brilliantly**. He made indescribably beautiful music on his nylon string classical guitar.

A3-5. **def**-i-nite-ly: Are you **definitely** sure that you locked the backdoor? Are you *certain beyond a question*? You need *to be sure* you locked it.

A3-6. de-**lib**-er-àte-ly: Did you **deliberately** knock over the chair or did you accidentally bump it. **Deliberately** means *on purpose*. Did you mean to do it? I hope not.

A3-7. **dif**-fer-ent-ly: Doctors treat different diseases **differently**. A medicine that will cure one disease often will not cure a different disease.

A3-8. dis-a-**bil**-i-ty: A **disability** is a *physical or mental condition that limits one's activities*. A blind person has a sight **disability** and a deaf person has a hearing **disability**.

A3-9. fun-dà-**men**-tal-ly: There are two **fundamentally** different ways to teach reading. The right way teaches phonics and the other teaches guessing. Mr. Potter teaches phonics, not guessing. They are *completely* different.

A3-10. im-**me**-di-àte-ly: John knew **immediately** that he needed to get his homework done. He knew *right away* that he could not go outside to play till it was all done.

A3-11. in-**def**-i-nite-ly. The shipwrecked sailors feared they were going to be stranded on the island **indefinitely**. They did not know how long it would be till a rescue boat would find them. The time was *not definite*.

A3-12. **mod**-er-àte-ly: The pizza was **moderately** hot. It was not real hot or real cold. It was just *in between*. Some would say it was just lukewarm.

A3-13. re-li-à-**bil**-i-ty: The **reliability** of our new car is not very high. We cannot *trust it to perform well*. **Reliability** is *a noun form of the adjective reliable*.

A3-14. **rest**-less-ly: The boy fidgeted in his chair **restlessly**. He could *not be still*. He kept moving because he was restless.

A3-15. **truth**-ful-ly: Did the witness to the accident speak **truthfully**. Did he *tell the whole truth about what really happened*?

A3-16. **won**-der-ful-ly: Jan sang **wonderfully** at the concert. Her voice was absolutely beautiful. She did a wonderful job singing all the difficult high notes in the cantata.

A3-17. Con-**nec**-ti-cut: Have you ever been to the state of **Connecticut**. It is a beautiful but cold state in the winter. Hartford is the capital.

A3-18. **ac**-cel-er-ate: A rocket ship has to **accelerate** to a very high speed to escape the gravitational field of the earth and put a satellite into orbit. To **accelerate** is *to move more quickly*.

A3-19. ac-**ces**-si-ble: The books in my office are easily **accessible**. It is *easy to get to them* since they are all on open bookshelves.

A3-20. ac-ci-**den**-tàl-ly: I **accidentally** left my lunch at home today. I did *not* leave it at home *on purpose*. It was an *unintentional accident*. I'll buy a sandwich at the local deli.

A3-21. ac-**com**-mò-date: The motel had to **accommodate** the cripple visitors by putting up a ramp to make it easier for them to get into the motel. The motel *took care of their needs*.

A3-22. ac-**cu**-mu-late: Linda knows how to **accumulate** a lot of books. She knows how *to collect* lots of wonderful books on all kinds of interesting subjects.

A3-23. ad-ò-**les**-cence: Mary is still in the **adolescence** stage of life. She *thinks and talks like a teenager*. Everybody passes through the **adolescence** stage on the way to becoming a responsible and productive adult.

Group A4: Wise Owl Polysyllables

A4-1. as-**sis**-tànce: I need some **assistance**. Can you *help* me? To assist means *to help by sharing in the work*. We should all try to be of **assistance** to those who need help.

A4-2. as-tro-**nom**-i-cal: The spaceship cost an **astronomical** amount of money. It cost *a lot* of money.

A4-3. at-**ten**-dànce: Joe's **attendance** at school was not very good. He missed a lot of days. He did not attend school like he should. **Attendance** is *to be present at a place, meeting, or function*. His teacher gave him makeup work so he wouldn't get behind.

A4-4. **brill**-iance: Albert Einstein showed a lot of **brilliance** when he discovered the Theory of Relativity. It was a brilliant scientific discovery by a *very smart* man.

A4-5. cer-e-**mo**-ni-al: The natives did a special **ceremonial** dance to celebrate the rich harvest of corn last year. They danced at a big ceremony.

A4-6. cer-**tif**-i-càte: Your teacher will give you a <u>WISE OWL Polysyllables **Certificate** of Completion</u> when you finish reading all the words in this book *to confirm in a formal statement* that you successfully completed the program.

A4-7. com-**mand**-ment: A **commandment** is a *rule or law* that everyone should keep. Brush your teeth before going to bed is a good **commandment** to follow.

A4-8. com-**mence**-ment: They had a **commencement** ceremony for the students graduating from high school. They call it a **commencement** because it is the *beginning* of a new phase in the students' lives.

A4-9. com-**men**-dà-ble: Janet did a **commendable** job fixing supper yesterday evening. She *deserved praise* for the delicious and nutritious supper she prepared.

A4-10. com-**mu**-ni-cate: Morse Code is one way to **communicate** with Amateur Radio. Mr. Potter is a high-speed code operator. His call sign is NG5W.

A4-11. **con**-cen-trate: To **concentrate** means to *focus your attention on one thing*. You have to learn to **concentrate** to make good grades in school.

A4-12. **con**-fer-ence: Johnny's parents had a **conference** with his teacher about his poor spelling grade. A **conference** is a *formal meeting for discussion*.

A4-13. **con**-fi-dent-ly: Alexis said **confidently** that she was ready to make an A+ on her spelling test. She was **certain** that she would get a good grade because she studied hard.

A4-14. con-**fine**-ment: The incorrigible prisoner was put in solitary **confinement**. His jail cell was isolated from the others so he couldn't cause anybody trouble.

A4-15. con-**fis**-cate: The government decided to **confiscate** Harvey's car because he was unable to pay his taxes. They had *authority to take it away* from him until he paid his taxes. He got a part time job to make enough money to pay his back taxes.

A4-16. con-**sid**-er-àte: Mark was **considerate** of the older people who got to the concert late. He gave them his seat so they would not have to stand. He was *nice to them*.

A4-17. con-**sol**-i-date: Henry decided to **consolidate** all his money. He took all his money out of his different bank accounts and *put them together* into one big bank account.

A4-18. **con**-stant-ly: Mr. Potter is **constantly** working to be the best reading teacher he can be. He is typing these polysyllables so YOU can become an advanced reader. He *never stops* working to help all his students read better.

A4-19. con-**sul**-tant: When Mr. Potter needs help teaching cursive handwriting, he contacts Mr. Randy Nelson, who is the best handwriting **consultant** in the United States. He is a *professional who gives expert advice.*

A4-20. con-**tam**-i-nate: Years ago a dangerous chemical called dioxin leaked into a town's water supply. It contaminated the water and made it dangerous to drink. To **contaminate** means *to add a poison to something we eat, drink, breathe, or touch.*

A4-21. con-**tes**-tant: One year Annie was a **contestant** in a nationwide cursive handwriting contest. When she won, they sent her a beautiful certificate. They also sent her a finely handcrafted German made fountain pen.

A4-22. con-ti-**nen**-tàl. The **Continental** United States includes all the states except Hawaii, which is actually a big island in the Pacific. Hawaii is not on the North American Continent. A continent is a *continuous mass of land.*

Group A5: Wise Owl Polysyllables

A5-1. con-**tin**-u-al-ly: It rained **continually** for three days. It *never stopped*, but continued on and on and on.

A5-2. con-tra-**dict**: Mr. Potter had to **contradict** the Educational Directors who said that first grade students cannot read polysyllables. He wrote Wise Owl Polysyllables to prove that he was right.

A5-3. con-**trib**-ute: Would you like to **contribute** a sports article about the Rising Sun Shiners' big win at the basketball game last Friday? **Contribute**, as used here, means *to provide an article for a newspaper*.

A5-4. **crit**-i-cal-ly: When you read **critically**, you read *carefully* to see if what you are reading is true and makes sense. We should read the newspaper **critically**.

A5-5. **del**-i-càte-ly: Be careful about touching the paper flowers because they are **delicately** made. It would be very *easy to damage* them.

A5-6. de-**scen**-dànt: I am a **descendant** of Walter G. Potter. He was my grandfather. My dad, Orson D. Potter, was the son of Walter, and I am the son of Orson. Who is your grandfather? Who is your dad?

A5-7. **dif**-fer-ence: Mr. Potter thinks learning polysyllables can make a big **difference** in your ability to read. You will read much better once you learn how to read lots of big words consisting of many syllables. It's easy if you read one syllable at a time.

A5-8. dif-fi-**cul**-ty: Some boys and girls have **difficulty** learning to read. Mr. Potter specializes in helping people of all ages to learn to read in spite of any *problem* they may have had learning to read.

A5-9. dis-con-**nect**: I need to **disconnect** my computer. I need *to unplug* it from the electric outlet. Dis- is a common prefix denoting reversal of an action.

A5-10. dis-**crim**-i-nate: Mr. Potter cannot **discriminate** colors very well. He has a color deficit or weakness that makes it *hard to distinguish* colors. It can be frustrating.

A5-11. dis-**tinct**-ly: Dr. Art Katt told his class that they needed to speak **distinctly** so people can understand them. It is important *to speak clearly and intelligibly*.

A5-12. ec-o-**nom**-i-cal: A bicycle is a very **economical** mode of transportation. It requires no gas or oil. It is *inexpensive* to get around on a bicycle.

A5-13. e-lec-**tric**-i-ty: **Electricity** is a form of energy that can run through wires to power our homes. Thomas Edison's invention of the electric light bulb was a great invention.

A5-14. e-lec-**tron**-ic: An **electronic** device *runs on electricity*. It takes electricity to run. A computer is a common **electronic** device.

A5-15. en-thu-si-**as**-tic: The Rising Sun Shiners' basketball players were very **enthusiastic** about the coming game. They were all *excited* about the game.

A5-16. **fran**-ti-cal-ly: The brave little girl **frantically** flagged down a passing trucker to get him to help her family. Her family was pinned in a car after a bad wreck. The little girl was *very excited and worried*. The trucker saved the day by prying open the doors.

A5-17. hys-**te**-ri-cal. The kids were **hysterical** when Jimmy yelled, "Snake!" They started screaming and running, but it was just a prank. He got in big trouble.

A5-18. in-ac-**ces**-si-ble: The bank keeps our money in a big vault. The money is **inaccessible** to anybody without the combination. They *cannot get to* our money.

A5-19. in-ci-**den**-tal-ly: Penicillin was discovered **incidentally** when Alexander Fleming was looking at a mold under a microscope. He was not looking for penicillin, he just *accidentally happened to find it while looking for something else.*

A5-20. in-con-**sis**-tent: The reports on the auto accident were **inconsistent**. They were *not consistent*. One report said the man fell asleep; the other, said he was distracted by his cell phone. The reports *did not agree*. The prefix in- means *not* in words like incredible and insincere.

A5-21. in-**cred**-i-ble: The animation in the movie was **incredible**. It was *hard to believe* that it was just a movie. It looked so real.

A5-22. in-**dict**-ment: The bank robber received an **indictment** for his part in masterminding the bank heist. He was *formally charged* and sent to jail.

Group A6: Wise Owl Polysyllables

A6-1. in-**dif**-fer-ence: Jim had an **indifference** as to who won the ball game. He was *unconcerned*; he *didn't care* who won. He was indifferent.

A6-2. in-**her**-i-tance: I have a beautiful gold pocket watch that is an **inheritance** from my father, who inherited it from his father. I will pass it on to my son.

A6-3. **in**-no-cent-ly: Johnny **innocently** dropped the rock on his sister's foot. It accidentally fell out of his slippery hands. He didn't mean to hurt her.

A6-4. in-**sis**-tence: Jane *begged and begged* for her mother to take her to the movies. Her **insistence** paid off because her mother eventually gave in and took her.

A6-5. in-ter-**fe**-rence: At the football game, the player illegally interfered with the pass. The referee said it was an **interference**. It cost his team several yards.

A6-6. math-e-**mat**-ics: **Mathematics** is defined as *the abstract science of number, quality, and space*. We are doing math when we solve a formula in algebra.

A6-7. ne-**ces**-si-tate: The wreck was so bad as to **necessitate** the use of the Jaws of Life to get Kathy out of the wrecked car. It was necessary to use the Jaws of Life to pry open the door. Amazingly she was not hurt.

A6-8. nu-**mer**-i-cal-ly: The scores were listed **numerically**. They were *listed in numerical order*. 1, 2, 3, 4 is numerical order. 8, 1, 16, 2 is not numerical order.

A6-9. re-**lo**-cate: Many farmers had to **relocate** when the Army started the Proving Grounds to test the weapons. They were very sad because they had *to move from their homes and farms and go to live somewhere else*. They were never allowed to move back.

A6-10. re-**luc**-tant-ly: Janet **reluctantly** agreed to go with her friends to the party. She *hesitated* to go with them because she was not sure if it would be any fun.

A6-11. re-**mem**-brance: I have a good **remembrance** of my childhood. I remember lots of fun things that I did with my brother on the old dairy farm.

A6-12. re-**sem**-blance: When they got done remodeling my room, it had no **resemblance** to the old room. It didn't resemble it at all. It *looked like* a brand new room.

A6-13. re-**sis**-tance: The criminal offered no **resistance** to being arrested. He let the police put the handcuffs on him and take him to jail without fighting. He did not resist them. To resist is to *refuse to obey*. **Resistance** is the *noun form for the verb resist*.

A6-14. sta-**tis**-tics: **Statistics** is the science of analyzing numerical data. **Statistics** analyzes a small group to see what the whole group is doing. Our librarian collects **statistics** on how many books each class is reading.

A6-15. sub-**scrib**-er: Mr. Potter is a **subscriber** to guitar magazines so he can learn what his favorite guitarist are playing. The magazines come to his house every month.

A6-16. suc-**cess**-ful-ly: Mr. Huron **successfully** taught biology to all his eleventh graders. All his students experienced success in learning the science that deals with living things.

A6-17. sym-**met**-ri-cal: Jan drew a beautiful heart. The two halves were **symmetrical**. They were *exactly the same*.

A6-18. tab-er-**nac**-le: A **tabernacle** is a *big tent* often used for worship.

A6-19. ta-**ble**-cloth: Katherine put a **tablecloth** on the table to protect the expensive wooden top. **Tablecloth** is a compound word.

A6-20. trans-con-ti-**nen**-tal: The **Transcontinental** Railroad went from one side of America all the way to the other side. It united the East with the West.

A6-21. tu-ber-cu-**lo**-sis: **Tuberculosis** is an *infectious bacterial disease especially of the lungs*.

A6-22. un-suc-**cess**-ful. Jim was **unsuccessful** in studying for his spelling test. He was *not successful*. He should study harder to be **successful** the next time.

Group B Symbol-to-Sound Relationships

or v p wh

Group B1 Wise Owl Polysyllables

B1-1. am-**bas**-sa-dor: The American **Ambassador** to Spain *represents the interests* of the United States to Spain. He lives in the U.S. Embassy in Spain.

B1-2. as-**sort**-ment: Most people like an **assortment** of chocolate. They like to buy *different kinds* of chocolate mixed up in a single box.

B1-3. Cal-i-**for**-ni-a: **California** is a beautiful state on the West Coast of the United States. There are lots of movie stars there. They also have delicious oranges.

B1-4. **com**-for-ta-ble: It is important to have a **comfortable** mattress on your bed if you expect to get a good night's sleep. They provide *physical ease and relaxation.*

B1-5. com-**mem**-o-rate: On the Fourth of July we **commemorate** Independence Day. We recall and show respect for the brave patriots who fought for the freedom and values we hold so dear.

B1-6. **com**-men-ta-tor: The news **commentator** made some startling comments about education on the news this evening. A commentator is *a person who makes comments on events or texts*. He said we need more phonics and cursive if all children are going to learn to read well.

B1-7. con-**for**-mi-ty: The boss said we need more **conformity** around here. We need everybody *to comply with the rules*. Everybody needs to obey the rules.

B1-8. con-**trac**-tor: Randy is a **contractor** who builds houses. He *provides workers and material* to build projects like houses and factories.

B1-9. con-**trib**-u-tor: A **contributor** is *a person who contributes things*. Sarah contributed an article entitled the "Baroque Classical Guitar" to a guitar magazine last month. She was a **contributor** to the magazine.

B1-10. **dem**-on-stra-tor: The **demonstrator** started a march to protest the failure of the schools to teach children the invaluable skill of cursive handwriting. Good luck!

B1-11. dis-**or**-der-ly: The school library was **disorderly**. There were books laying around all over the place in a *disorganized* mess. They were *not in order*.

B1-12. en-**force**-ment: A policeman is responsible for the **enforcement** of the law. They make sure people obey the law.

B1-13. **for**-mi-dà-ble: The Rams were **formidable** opponents on the football field. They were *respected because they played so well*.

B1-14. hence-**forth**: Henceforth means *from now on*. Mr. Potter said that **henceforth** he would teach sentence diagramming and the parts of speech to all his students.

B1-15. his-**tor**-i-cal: Washington is a very **historical** city. You can learn a lot about the history of America by visiting the monuments and government buildings.

B1-16. **il**-lus-tra-tor: Many children's books are illustrated by an artist. An **illustrator** is *a person who draws or creates pictures for books.* –or is a suffix indicating a person performing action.

B1-17. im-mor-**tal**-i-ty: **Immortality** is *the ability to live forever.* The Gods of the Greeks and Romans were said to be immortal. They were thought to live forever and never die.

B1-18. in-**struc**-tor: An **instructor** is *someone who teaches.* Mr. Huron was a great physics and chemistry **instructor**. He taught hands-on science in his science lab.

B1-19. in-tro-**duc**-to-ry: Mr. Hazel Loring's Blend Phonics is an **introductory** reading course. It introduces reading with phonics to students who are just learning to read.

B1-20. mem-o-**ran**-dum: The principal wrote a **memorandum** telling everyone that the ball game had been postponed because of rain. A memorandum is *a note made for future use.*

B1-21. or-na-**men**-tal: There was an **ornamental** fountain in the middle of the town. It was *highly decorated* with statues of famous people from the area.

B1-21. or-na-**men**-tal: There was an **ornamental** fountain in the middle of the town. It was *highly decorated* with statues of famous people from the area.

B1-23. **scorn**-ful-ly: Jimmy spoke **scornfully** of Jerry's attempt to break the school high jump record, until Jerry broke it. To speak scornfully is *to express contempt*.

B1-24. **nu**-me-ra-tor: A **numerator** is *the number on the top line over a fraction*. In the fraction 2/3, the number 2 is the numerator.

Group B2 Wise Owl Polysyllables

B2-1. **stub**-born-ly: Mary's mule **stubbornly** refused to move until she offered him some corn. Adding the suffix –ly to stubborn turns it into an adverb.

B2-2. sub-**or**-di-nate: Jimmy was a **subordinate** officer in the club. He ranked under the president in authority. The prefix sub- means *under*.

B2-3. ter-ri-**tor**-i-al: Some dogs can be very **territorial**. They do not want people on their owner's property. Territorial relates to a *particular territory, district, or locality*.

B2-4. un-**com**-for-ta-bly: Julie's new shoes were **uncomfortably** tight. They were *not comfortable* because they were very tight.

B2-5. un-cor-**rec**-ted: Mr. Potter does not want any incorrectly spelled words in the books he publishes. He does not want to leave them **uncorrected**.

B2-6. ab-**bre**-vi-a-ted: One day Mr. Potter **abbreviated** his name. His full name is Donald Leroy Potter. His initials are D. L. P. What are your initials? To abbreviate is *to shorten a word, phrase, or text.*

B2-7. ad-**vance**-ment: Students who study WISE OWL Polysyllables always make great **advancement** in their reading ability. To advance is *to move forward in a purposeful way.* **Advancement** is *the noun form of to advance.*

B2-8. ad-ver-**tise**-ment: An **advertisement** is *a notice or announcement in public media promoting a product or service.* I saw an **advertisement** for Blend Phonics on the Internet last week.

B2-9. al-**ter**-na-tive: When the mudslide destroyed the regular road to the top of the mountain, we had no **alternative** but to take *another route.* We took a *different road* that went to the *same place.* It was an alternate route.

B2-10. be-**nev**-o-lent: Dad is a member of a **benevolent** society. The society *helps people* by teaching the knowledge and skills they need to read and make a good living.

B2-11. con-**sec**-u-tive: 1, 2, 3, 4 are **consecutive** numbers since they *follow each other in order one after the other.* ABCDE are **consecutive** letters.

B2-12. con-**struc**-tive: Robert had a **constructive** idea about how to build a clubhouse in a tree in his backyard. He had some very *useful ideas* about how to build it.

B2-13. con-**tri**-vance: An automobile is a good example of a **contrivance**. It requires a lot of *skill to build and serves a particular purpose*. **Contrivance** comes from contrive, to make or build.

B2-14. **con**-tro-ver-sy: There was a great **controversy** at my school over who was the fastest runner in sixth grade. The kids *disagreed* about it until John beat Jim in a race.

B2-15. con-**ver**-ti-ble: Mary's car is a red **convertible**. She puts the top up when it rains and down when it is sunny. **Convertible** means *able to be converted or changed*.

B2-16. **cul**-ti-va-ted: Billy **cultivated** flowers in his garden. He *broke up the land and prepared it for planting* his flowers.

B2-17. **cum**-u-la-tive: The **cumulative** effect of two years without any rain was devastating on the crops and the cattle that depended on them for food. It *added up*.

B2-18. **dec**-o-ra-tive: Wanita bought a highly **decorative** fountain pen. It has a detailed picture of a beautiful mountain scene etched on the barrel.

B2-19. de-**struc**-tive: The tornado that swept through the local forest was very **destructive**, uprooting trees and destroying crops. It *destroyed* the forest.

B2-20. dis-**cov**-er-er: Christopher Columbus was the **discoverer** of the New World. He and his brave sailors discovered it after sailing across the Atlantic Ocean from Spain in their little sailing ships.

B2-21. dis-**tinc**-tive: One thing **distinctive** about Mr. Potter's teaching is that he teaches all his student to write fluent cursive handwriting. That is one thing that distinguishes him from a lot of other teachers.

B2-22. ef-**fec**-tive-ly: To read **effectively** you must learn to read all the syllables in polysyllable words. A polysyllable is a word that has more than one syllable.

B2-23. in-ad-**ver**-tent: John didn't plan to go to Boston. His arrival was **inadvertent**. He didn't plan it. It *just happened* when he took a wrong turn on the Interstate.

B2-24. de-**nom**-i-na-tor: The denominator in the fraction 2/3 is three. It is *the number on the bottom of a fraction*.

Group B3 Wise Owl Polysyllables

B3-1. in-di-**vid**-u-al: **Individual** effort is very important if you plan to become a good reader. You have *to work hard yourself* and do the best you can.

B3-2. in-**ev**-i-ta-ble: The gaping hole made by the enormous iceberg in the side of the Titanic made it **inevitable** that the mighty ship would sink to the bottom of the cold Atlantic Ocean. It was *certain* to sink.

B3-3. in-**for**-ma-tive: Mr. Blumenfeld published an **informative** paper on teaching reading with phonics and cursive handwriting. It *contains a lot of information*.

B3-4. in-**stinc**-tive-ly: The German Shepherd dog knew **instinctively** to protect its owner from the robbers. He chased them *without thinking or having to be commanded*.

B3-5. in-**val**-u-a-ble: Miss Geraldine Rodgers gave Mr. Potter some **invaluable** advice on how to teach reading. She pointed out to him the *great value* of teaching phonics-first.

B3-6. in-**vest**-ment: If you invest your money early, you may have a lot of money when you retire. Just make an **investment** in something that has great returns.

B3-7. in-**vin**-ci-ble: King David was an **invincible** warrior. He was so powerful and blessed by The LORD that *nobody could hurt or defeat him*.

B3-8. in-**volve**-ment: Good parents always have a strong **involvement** in education. They are involved in helping their children learn as much as they possibly can.

B3-9. lo-co-**mo**-tive: The powerful diesel **locomotive** can pull a lot of heavily laden railroad cars up the tall mountain. The **locomotive** is *the part of the train that pulls the cars*.

B3-10. **love**-li-est: Sherry is the **loveliest** girl in the whole class. She is the *prettiest and most attractive*. She also has an inward, hidden beauty that comes from being kind and considerate.

B3-11. nev-er-the-**less**: Julie meant well; **nevertheless** she did manage to upset her best friend Susie when she forgot to invite her to her birthday party.

B3-12. **rel**-à-tive-ly: Jimmy was rather small **relatively** speaking. He was short *compared to the other* students in the class.

B3-13. se-**lec**-tive-ly: Mr. Potter chooses phonics programs very **selectively**. He looks at them all and chooses only the best programs like Reading Made Easy with Blend Phonics.

B3-14. sev-en-**teenth**: **Seventeenth** is a *ordinal number meaning one more than sixteenth*. It is abbreviated 17th. The **seventeenth** century was a great age of exploration.

B3-15. suc-**ces**-sive: The Shiners were on a winning streak. Last week's victory was their 12th **successive** win. They won 12 basketball games in a row.

B3-16. them-**selves**: The boys taught **themselves** to communicate in Morse Code. They learned from a book *without help from anybody*.

B3-17. un-**fa**-vor-a-ble: They had to cancel the football game because of the **unfavorable** weather. The game was called off because the weather did *not favor* the game. They couldn't play because the field was too wet.

B3-18. u-ni-**ver**-sal-ly: English is almost **universally** known. *Everybody* knows some English.

B3-19. u-ni-**ver**-si-ty: Practically all Mr. Potter's tutoring students will study at the **university** because he teaches them what they need to know to do advanced studies. A **university** is *a school for advanced studies* like psychology, physics, music, history, etc.

B3-20. vin-**dic**-tive: People who are **vindictive** always *seek revenge* when someone does something mean or harmful to them. They want *to get back at them by doing something just as bad*. Mr. Potter tells us that two wrongs don't make a right.

B3-21. vis-i-**bil**-i-ty: Be careful when you drive in the fog because the fog lowers your **visibility**. **Visibility** is *the ability to see or be seen*. Fog makes it hard to see where you are going.

B3-22. Mis-sis-**sip**-pi: The **Mississippi** River is *the second longest river in the United States*. **Mississippi** is also *the name of one of the southern states in the United States*.

B3-23. Penn-syl-**van**-i-a. The State of **Pennsylvania** was founded in 1682 by William Penn. It became one of the original thirteen colonies. Its state insect is the firefly.

Group B4 Wise Owl Polysyllables

B4-1. ac-**cep**-ta-ble: Harvey wrote an **acceptable** paper for his English class. His teachers said it was *good enough to be accepted* for a grade.

B4-2. an-**tic**-i-pate: Mr. Potter **anticipates** that all his tutoring students will learn to read well. He *expects* them to read well once they learn their phonics.

B4-3. ap-**pen**-di-ces: There are some neat phonics charts in the **appendices** to Mr. Fletcher's *Shortcut to Reading: Teacher's Manual*. It shows how to spell all 44 English speech sounds.

B4-4. ap-**pli**-ca-ble: The laws of gravity are **applicable** everywhere in the universe. They *apply to* everything in the universe that has mass. Gravity makes apples fall to the earth.

B4-5. ap-**pren**-tice: Jaxon Santos was Mr. Potter's **apprentice** when he was in first-grade. He was *learning* to teach *by working under direction* from Mr. Potter.

B4-6. ap-**pro**-pri-ate: We should always do **the appropriate** thing at school. **Appropriate** means *doing the right thing at the right time*. It is always **appropriate** to listen well.

B4-7. **blue**-prints: Raymond learned how to read **blueprints** in drafting class. **Blueprints** are *like a map that tells you about the design of a house, structure, or machine.*

B4-8. ca-pa-**bil**-i-ty: The **capability** of Mrs. Hazel Loring's <u>Reading Made Easy with Blend Phonics for First Grade</u> to teach reading has been clearly demonstrated. It is *capable* of teaching children, teens, and adults to read well.

B4-9. com-**pat**-i-ble: The ink cartridges in a Jefferson Fountain Pen and a Washington Fountain Pen are **compatible**. An ink cartridge made for one will work in the other. They are interchangeable.

B4-10. **com**-pen-sate: To **compensate** for a broken right hand, Jerry had to learn to write with his left hand. To compensate is *to make up for a loss by doing something else*.

B4-11. com-**pet**-i-tive: Mr. Potter's grandson is very **competitive** in motor sports. He rides a fast KTM motocross bike and wins a lot of races.

B4-12. com-**plete**-ly: The furniture in Jenny's room was **completely** covered with dust. Her window was left open during the dust storm, and all the furniture was *totally* covered with a thick layer of dust. She cleaned it with a good cleaner and waxed it to a brilliant shine.

B4-13. **com**-pli-ca-ted: Jimmy's computer program was so **complicated** that he ended up with over 10,000 lines of complex computer code.

B4-14. **com**-pli-ment: Mr. Potter paid his first grade teacher a good **compliment** when he said she was a great teacher. He said great things about Mrs. Pearl Monroe.

B4-15. **com**-pre-hend: If you can't **comprehend** what a sentence is saying, just look up the words you don't know in a dictionary. To **comprehend** is *to understand*.

B4-16. com-pre-**hen**-sive: Mr. Potter teaches a **comprehensive** reading program that teaches handwriting, speech sounds, phonics, vocabulary, spelling, and grammar. His program is **complete**, with nothing missing.

B4-17. **com**-pro-mise: Mary and Sarah both wanted to be first in line to lunch. They solved the dispute by deciding to take turns. They made a **compromise**.

B4-18. com-**pul**-so-ry: Education in the United States is **compulsory**. Everyone is *required by law* to attend a school of some kind. The school can be public, private, or homeschool.

B4-19. **con**-tem-plate: To **contemplate** is *to think about something carefully for a long time*. Mr. Potter likes to **contemplate** how much fun his students will have reading great stories once he has taught them to read well with phonics.

B4-20. cor-res-**pon**-dent: Ernie Powell was a war **correspondent** during World War II. He wrote articles for newspapers telling the world about the brave men who won that war and saved the world from Nazi domination.

B4-21. de-**pen**-da-ble: Bryson's new fountain pen is very **dependable**. You *can depend on it* to write every time. Make sure you have extra ink cartridges handy at all times.

B4-22. de-**plor**-a-ble: The house was in **deplorable** shape. It had fallen into really *bad shape* after the owners abandoned the house. The windows were broken, the roof leaked, and the doors were missing. **Deplorable** means *something is in shockingly bad condition*.

B4-23. **des**-per-ate-ly: The brave firemen **desperately** tried to save the little girl from the burning house. They *made a great effort* to save her by breaking down the door and rushing through the blazing fire to carry her to safety.

Group B5 Wise Owl Polysyllables

B5-1. **des**-pi-ca-ble: Mr. Potter thinks it is **despicable** to ask children to memorize sight-words. He *absolutely hates it* because he believes memorizing sight-words can make it hard for children to learn to read properly without guessing.

B5-2. de-**vel**-op-ment: The **development** of the modern airplane began with the flight of the Wright Brothers at Kitty Hawk. Their slow propeller driven biplane has developed into the fast, highflying jets of today. Airplane design improved step by step.

B5-3. dip-lo-**mat**-ic: The United States has good **diplomatic** relations with England. The two nations get along real well. Their diplomats work together for the common good.

B5-4. dis-ap-**prov**-al: My dad **disapproved** of me riding my bicycle without a helmet. He said he *did not approve* of me riding helmetless because I might fall off and hurt my head.

B5-5. **dis**-ci-pline: The teacher had to **discipline** the students who were throwing paper in class. He made them stay after school and clean the whole school building. **Discipline** is *the practice of training people to obey rules using punishment to correct disobedience.*

B5-6. en-cy-clo-**pe**-di-a: Mr. Potter has a beautiful set of the 1911 **Encyclopedia** Britannica in his office. An **encyclopedia** contains *informative articles on many topics that are usually listed in alphabetical order so they are easy to locate.*

B5-7. **en**-ter-prise: An **enterprise** is *a project that requires a lot of effort to complete.* The construction of a tall skyscraper is a good example of an **enterprise** because it is very difficult to design and requires a lot of effort to build.

B5-8. hos-pi-**tal**-i-ty: Mrs. Walton is given to **hospitality**. She is *very friendly to strangers and guests*. She welcomes them into her house to feed and take care of them.

B5-9. im-**plic**-it-ly: I trusted Alexis **implicitly** when she told me she had not taken my fountain pen. She was a girl that could be trusted to tell the truth. I *trusted* her *completely*.

B5-10. im-**por**-tance: Parents understand the **importance** of learning to read. They understand the *value* of reading in order for their children to do well in school and life.

B5-11. im-**pos**-si-ble: It is **impossible** to get to the moon without a powerful rocket ship. The brilliant rocket scientist Werner Von Braun was the chief designer of the powerful Saturn V Rocket that put the first men on the moon. **Impossible** means *it cannot be done*.

B5-12. im-p**rac**-ti-cal: It is **impractical** to run a foot race in high heel shoes. The heels make it much harder to run fast without falling and hurting oneself. They are *not practical*.

B5-13. im-**pres**-sive: Mr. Horton said it was **impressive** to see Mr. Potter's first grade tutoring students reading the Hobbit. He said, "I am really impressed to see them reading such a hard book!" Mr. Potter explained that the kids use a dictionary for the hard words.

B5-14. im-**pris**-on-ment: The car thief was sentenced to one year **imprisonment**. He will be *locked up behind bars in prison* for a whole year. I hope he learns his lesson.

B5-15. im-**prove**-ment: The workout room in John's house was a great **improvement**. It *made it better*. Now he can stay in shape at home without having to drive across town to the health gym.

B5-16. in-ap-**pro**-pri-åte: In America it is **inappropriate** to drive on the left side of the road. It could cause an accident. It is *not appropriate* or safe. We drive on the right side in the USA.

B5-17. in-com-**pat**-i-ble: The ink cartridges for a Cross Fountain Pen are *not compatible* with the cartridges for a Waterman Fountain Pen. Since they are **incompatible**, the ink cartridges will only work in the brand of pen for which they were designed.

B5-18. in-**com**-pe-tent: The town boy was **incompetent** to milk a cow until the country boy showed him how to do it. He *did not have the necessary skills* until the country boy showed him how to do it. Now he is competent. **Incompetent** means *not competent*.

B5-19. in-com-**plete**: Joan forgot to do her spelling yesterday. The teacher said her spelling work was **incomplete**. The prefix –in in incomplete means *not*. Incomplete = *not complete*.

B5-20. in-com-pre-**hen**-si-ble: Quantum Physics is **incomprehensible** to Physicists. They *cannot comprehend or understand it* fully. Quantum Physics tells us that particles behave differently when they are observed than when they are not observed. The suffix –in means *not,* so **incomprehensible** means *not comprehensible.*

B5-21. in-de-**pen**-dence: Mr. Weber values his **independence**. He is an independent contractor and works for himself. He *does not depend on anybody*.

B5-22. in-dis-**pen**-sa-ble: Reading is an **indispensable** skill. It is *absolutely necessary* to be able to read well in order be successful and happy in our modern, technologically advanced world.

B5-23. in-**ter**-pre-ter: Javier is a Spanish **interpreter**. He can tell you in English what Spanish people are saying in Spanish. Would you like to be an **interpreter** someday?

Group B6 Wise Owl Polysyllables

B6-1. ma-**nip**-u-late: To **manipulate** a fountain pen properly you have to have a proper tripod grip. To *handle* a pen *skillfully* you have to learn a good grip.

B6-2. **man**-u-script: A **manuscript** is *a book, document or piece of music written by hand rather than typed*. All books were manuscripts until the invention of the printing press.

B6-3. met-ro-**pol**-i-tan:. A metropolis is a very large and densely populated city. Dallas is a metropolis with a large **metropolitan** area. *Lots of people live and work there.*

B6-4. **mi**-cro-scope: Ronald got a **microscope** for Christmas. He put pond water on a slide and discovered that it was full of little swimming animals. A **microscope** is *an optical instrument for viewing very small objects*.

B6-5. op-por-**tu**-ni-ty: Julie had an **opportunity** to make a higher grade in biology class by turning in an extra paper. The teacher *made it possible* for her to get a better grade.

B6-6. op-**pres**-sive: **The oppressive** dictator unjustly made life very hard and restrictive for the people living in the country. He oppressed them with hard labor, working far underground in the dark, damp, and dangerous mines.

B6-7. **op**-ti-mis-tic: Mr. Potter is **optimistic** that someday all first-graders will learn to read with phonics-first so they can all be good readers. Mr. Potter is *hopeful and confident about the future* of reading instruction in America.

B6-8. **pa**-tri-o-tis-m: **Patriotism** is taught at our school. A patriot is a person who vigorously supports his or her country against enemies or detractors.

B6-9. pe-**des**-tri-an. **Pedestrians** have to be careful when walking across the street. A pedestrian is *anybody who is walking along a road or in a developed area.*

B6-10. per-**for**-mance: Sarah gave an outstanding **performance** with her violin at the Rambling Rose Concert. She played a popular country fiddle tune.

B6-11. pe-ri-**od**-i-cal: Classical Guitar is a popular guitar **periodical** that comes every month. It is a great monthly magazine. Periodicals are *magazines or newspapers that are published at regular intervals.*

B6-12. **per**-ma-nent-ly: Be careful with pens that use permanent ink. They can **permanently** damage your shirt with a mark that *will be there forever since it can't be removed*.

B6-13. per-**mis**-si-ble: It is not **permissible** to talk on a cell phone at the movies. Nobody has permission to talk on the phone and interrupt people during a movie.

B6-14. per-se-**ver**-ance: It takes a lot of **perseverance** to teach some children to read. **Perseverance** means that you are *able and willing to keep doing something despite difficulty or delay until success is achieved*. You never give up.

B6-15. per-**sis**-tence: It takes a lot of **persistence** on the part of a good teacher to make sure all the children learn to read well. Some learn to read faster than others, but all can learn to read if the teacher has **persistence** and *never gives up in spite of difficulty*.

B6-16. per-son-**al**-i-ty: Ruth had a wonderful **personality**. She was always happy, and she made everybody around her feel happy. I think you have a wonderful **personality**!

B6-17. **per**-son-al-ly: Kenny thanked Mrs. Pearl Monroe **personally** for teaching him to read so well at the Cass Union School. He thanked her *himself*.

B6-18. per-**spec**-tive: Mr. Macintyre teaches the Seven Elements of **Perspective** in his drawing class. **Perspective** means *representing three-dimensional objects with two-dimensional drawings*.

B6-19. per-**sua**-sive: Helen gave a **persuasive** speech. It was a *convincing* speech that helped us see the importance of recycling our bottles, cans, paper, and electronic devices.

B6-20. **pes**-ti-lence: A **pestilence** is *a fatal disease that affects a lot of people*. The Black Plague was a terrible **pestilence** that killed a lot of people in the Middle Ages.

B6-21. **pos**-i-tive-ly: Miss Rodgers is **positively** certain that teaching sight-words can cause reading difficulties. She is *totally convinced* that it causes a lot of problems with reading.

B6-22. pos-si-**bil**-i-ty: The **possibility** of making an 100% on your next spelling test is good if you study hard. The *chances* are excellent.

B6-23. **prac**-ti-cal-ly: **Practically** everybody knows that the Wright brothers invented the first heavier than air flying machine. *Almost* everybody knows that.

Group B7 Wise Owl Polysyllables

B7-1. **prec**-e-dence: Reading instruction is so important that it should take **precedence** over every other subject in the first grade curriculum. **Precedence** means *one thing is more important than anything else*.

B7-2. **pred**-e-ces-sor: Mr. Cates was my predecessor in the Spanish department. He taught Spanish there before me. He was my **predecessor**, and I was his successor.

B7-3. pre-**dic**-a-ment: The kids were in a bad **predicament** when they got lost in the forest and couldn't find their way home. A **predicament** is *a difficult situation*.

B7-4. **pref**-er-ence: Randy had a **preference** for dark chocolate. He preferred dark chocolate to milk chocolate. Which kinds of chocolate do you like best?

B7-5: pre-his-**tor**-ic: The fierce Tyrannosaurs Rex was a **prehistoric** animal because it lived before men started writing history. **Prehistoric** refers to *anything before men started keeping written records*. Would you like to meet a T-Rex?

B7-6: **prin**-ci-pal-ly: Mr. Potter is **principally** a reading teacher, but he can also teach guitar, art, exercise, and electronics. He is *mainly* a reading teacher, but he can teach other things.

B7-7. prob-à-**bil**-i-ty: The weather station said there is a 50% **probability** of rain today. The *likelihood* of it raining or not raining is the same.

B7-8. pro-**duc**-tive: Carroll was very **productive** in class today. He got all his work done so he will not have any homework this evening.

B7-9. re-**cep**-ta-cle: We should put our trash in a trash **receptacle** and not throw it on the ground. A **receptacle** is *an object or space used to contain something*.

B7-10. rep-re-**sen**-ta-tive: Mr. Foster is our *representative* to the state legislature. He represents our wishes in the state senate. He *speaks for us*.

B7-11. re-**spec**-ta-ble: Joan is a very **respectable** young lady. She always *does what is good and proper*. People respect her a lot because of the values she holds and the life she lives.

B7-12. re-**spon**-si-bil-i-ty: It is your **responsibility** to study for your spelling test, but it is also your teacher's **responsibility** to teach you the meaning and spelling of the words.

B7-13. sim-**plic**-i-ty: **Simplicity** is very important in teaching. Good teachers simplify learning by teaching complex skills, such as algebra, step by step.

B7-14. spe-**cif**-i-cal-ly: Mr. Albert Potter **specifically** told his class to do all their written work with a fountain pen. He told them in *precise and clear language* exactly what he wanted.

B7-15. su-per-in-**ten**-dent: The **Superintendent** of Schools has a very important job. A good **superintendent** makes sure teachers have a good curriculum and good training.

B7-16. su-pe-**ri**-or-i-ty: The **superiority** of the phonics method for teaching reading over the look-and-say method is obvious to those who have studied the two methods. Phonics is *far better*. **Superiority** is the *state of being superior or better*.

B7-17. su-per-**vi**-sor: A **supervisor** is *a person who watches over a person or an activity*. Mr. Potter is a **supervisor** of reading instruction. He *watches over* the reading teachers to make sure that they teach spelling patterns.

B7-18. **sup**-ple-ment: A **supplement** is *something that completes or enhances something else when added to it*. A good vitamin **supplement** provides the vitamins that might be missing in our regular diet.

B7-19. sus-**cep**-ti-ble: Students who memorize sight-words are often **susceptible** to the guessing habit. They are *likely or liable* to have their reading harmed by the sight-words.

B7-20. sym-pa-**thet**-ic: Mr. Potter is not **sympathetic** toward teachers who teach sight-words. He does *not approve* of their harmful teaching methods.

Group B8 Wise Owl Polysyllables

B8-1. **wheel**-bar-row: A **wheelbarrow** is *a small cart with two handles and a single wheel on the front for moving things that are too heavy or awkward to carry by hand*. Every gardener needs a **wheelbarrow**.

B8-2. **whence**: Bilbo eventually returned to the place **whence** he had come after he helped to rescue the gold from Smaug the dragon. He lived in the Shire *from which* he commenced his famous adventure.

B8-3. **mean**-while: Jimmy hopes to go to college when he graduates from high school, **meanwhile** he is working to get good grades so he can get accepted into a good college. **Meanwhile** indicates the *time between two events*.

B8-4. **whale**: The novel, Moby Dick by Herman Melville, is the most famous **whale** story ever written. I hope you read it someday. A whale is a very *large marine mammal*.

B8-5. **whiff**: Mary caught a **whiff** of the beautiful roses. She *smelled them briefly* and liked the wonderful aroma.

B8-6. **where**-u-pon: Mr. Potter published Mrs. Hazel Loring's Reading Made Easy with Blend Phonics for First Grade in 2003, **whereupon** many teachers got copies and starting having greater success than ever teaching reading. Whereupon means *immediately after which*.

B8-7. **whirl**-wind: A strong **whirlwind** can be destructive. It is a *revolving, funnel shaped cloud* that picks up objects lying on the ground and tosses them around.

B8-8. **where**-a-bouts: Johnny's **whereabouts** was unknown for a long time. It turns out that he was visiting his uncle in Washington. Whereabouts is *the place where someone or something is*.

B8-9. what-so-**ev**-er: I have no doubt **whatsoever** that men and women will someday fly to Mars. I have no doubt *at all*.

B8-10. **whip**ped: Do you like **whipped** cream on your strawberry pie? **Whipped** cream is cream that has been *whipped into froth.*

B8-11. **an**-y-where: **Anywhere** you go, you will find kids who need good reading instruction. **Anywher**e is a compound word meaning *in or to any place.*

B8-12. **where**-with-al: Sam did not have the **wherewithal** to publish his book. He did not have the *money or means to reach his goal.*

B8-13. **whis**-per: You should never talk above a **whisper** in a library so you will not bother people who are reading. You should *speak very softly using your breath but not your vocal chords.*

B8-14. **whirl**-pool: A whirlpool is *rapidly rotating water in a river or sea that can suck things down into the whirling water.* They can be deadly to swimmers.

B8-15. where-**by**: Samuel Morse invented a code **whereby** people could communicate with mere dots and dashes. It is called the Morse Code. **Whereby** means *by which.*

B8-16. **whis**-tle: It is good to *whistle* while you work, but you might not want to **whistle** during history class!

B8-17. **where**-fore: **Wherefore** did you decide to write a novel about the Civil War. *For what reason* did you decide to write it?

B8-18. **whim**-si-cal: The teacher had a **whimsical** sense of humor. He liked to joke with his students. He asked, "Why do spiders do well at computers?" Answer: "They love the Web."

B8-19. **Sòme**-where: Betty told Angie that she had seen her before **somewhere**. It turns out that Angie had seen Betty at a ball game last year. **Somewhere** means *in or to some place*.

B8-20. whim: Nate was on his way to school when he decided on a **whim** to go swimming. He could not explain to his teacher his *sudden and unexpected change of mind*.

B8-21. **whet**-stone: Boy Scouts learn to sharpen their knives and hatches with a whetstone, which is a *find-grained stone for sharpening cutting tools*.

B8-22. **no**-where: Joan's art book was **nowhere** to be found. It was *not anywhere* to be found.

B8-23. whip-poor-**will**: Mr. Potter used to listen to the **whippoorwill** on the Indiana dairy farm where he was raised. A **whippoorwill** is a bird with a distinctive call.

B8-24. **white**-wash. Mr. Potter's dad was a dairy farmer. He used to whitewash the barn walls. He painted the walls white with *a solution of lime and water*.

Group C Symbol-to-Sound Relationships

ar (a r)   ng   sh   ai   ay   igh   k   ck
ur   ir   wor   j   ew   ould   gn   x

Group C1 Wise Owl Polysyllables

C1-1. an-ni-**ver**-sa-ry: Johnny and Anna celebrated their eighth **anniversary** last week. They have been married for eight years. **Anniversary** is *the date on which a couple was married in a previous year*.

C1-2. ap-**pa**-rent-ly: **Apparently** more kids liked Bears of Blue River than The Voyages of Dr. Doolittle, at least it *appears* that they did from the number of books they read last year.

C1-3. a-**ris**-to-crat: Julia was a peasant woman but Juana was an **aristocrat** of noble birth. Juana was a *noble person of the court* and Julia was a poor commoner of lowly birth.

C1-4. a-**rith**-me-tic: **Arithmetic** is an elementary school *subject dealing with counting and calculating with numbers*, including adding, subtraction, multiplication, and division.

C1-5. **care**-less-ly: If you write your numbers **carelessly** when doing arithmetic, you will often get the wrong answer. You need to write all your numbers with great care.

C1-6. **cat**-er-pil-lar: A **caterpillar** was happy quite, until a toad in fun, asked, "Pray tell, which foot comes after which?" This worked her mind to such a pitch; she lay distracted in the ditch considering how to run.

C1-7. **com**-men-ta-ry: Robert wrote an editorial **commentary** on Dr. Fleming's discovery of penicillin. He *explained how* Fleming accidentally discovered it.

C1-8. **com**-pa-ra-ble: Apples and oranges are **comparable** in that they are both healthy fruit. **Comparable** is used of *persons or things able to be likened to one another* in some way. Apples and oranges are both healthy fruits.

C1-8. **com**-pa-ra-ble: Apples and oranges are **comparable** in that they are both healthy fruit. **Comparable** is used of *persons or things able to be likened to one another* in some way. Apples and oranges are both healthy fruits.

C1-10. com-**part**-ment: Dad's toolbox has a different **compartment** for each kind of tool. Each tool has a different *section* so they don't get mixed together.

C1-11. **com**-ple-men-ta-ry: Phonics, spelling, reading, and handwriting are **complementary**. They *combine and enhance each other* to help students read and spell better.

C1-12. de-**part**-ment: The music **department** at our school teaches violin and piano. It is just *one part* of the school's total educational program.

C1-13. con-**tem**-po-rar-y: **Contemporary** means *living or occurring at the same time.* Sir Winston Churchill and Franklin D. Roosevelt were **contemporaries** that lead the Free World to victory during the Second World War.

C1-14. el-e-**men**-ta-ry: Learning to read is an important part of an **elementary** education. **Elementary** is related to *the rudimentary aspect of a subject.*

C1-15. em-**barr**-ass-ment: People who do not learn how to read often experience **embarrassment** when asked to read in public. They *feel ashamed* when asked to read aloud. Poor readers of all ages can benefit from a strong phonics reading program.

C1-16. mo-men-**tar**-i-ly: Marina **momentarily** paused when her mother asked her if she wanted to go to tutoring with Mr. Potter. She thought *for a short period of time* and then said, "Why, of course! I would love to go."

C1-17. nec-es-**sar**-i-ly: It is not **necessarily** true that a lot of money makes people happier. Mr. Potter's dad said that money did not **necessarily** have anything to do with true happiness. "You can't buy true happiness with money," he would always say.

C1-18. or-din-**ar**-i-ly: **Ordinarily** I would take my truck to work, but today I decided to do something different. I *usually* go to work in my truck, but today I rode my bicycle.

C1-19. pa-**ren**-the-sis: *A word, clause, or sentences inserted as an explanation into a passage that is grammatically complete without it* is called a **parenthesis**. A pair of round brackets ( ) are used to mark it off. Let's play (run around) outside.

C1-20. **par**-lia-ment: We got to visit the English **Parliament** when we visited England. The Parliament makes the laws for the British people.

C1-21. par-**tic**-i-pate: Chase had a great time **participating** in the Motor Cross Nationals in Anaheim, California. He *got to take part* in the televised race. He had fun hobnobbing with some of the finest riders in the history of motocross.

C1-22. par-**tic**-u-lar: Mr. Potter is very **particular** about the reading programs that he teaches. He insists that phonics-first is the *only correct way* to teach beginning reading.

C1-23. pe-cu-li-**ar**-i-ty: John had an odd **peculiarity** about the way he held his pencil. He insisted on holding it like a screwdriver until Mr. Potter showed him the correct way.

C1-24. **just**-i-fi-able. It is not **justifiable** to spend more money than you make. You will soon run out of money if you spend more than you make. It cannot be justified.

Group C2 Wise Owl Polysyllables

C2-1. per-pen-**dic**-u-lar: Maria's teacher showed her how to use a protractor to draw a **perpendicular** line. She drew it *90 degrees from the baseline, straight up and down.*

C2-2. pop-u-**lar**-i-ty: The American Astronauts that landed on the moon enjoyed a lot of **popularity** when they returned safely to the earth. They were *admired and liked by a lot of people.* There was even a parade in New York City to honor the brave astronauts.

C2-3. pre-**lim**-i-nar-y: Mr. Potter gives a **preliminary** test to determine exactly what reading skills his tutoring students need to be taught. This test is preliminary to everything else, it *comes before everything else.*

C2-4. **sep**-a-rate-ly: Each child is expected to do his or her work **separately**. They do it *by themselves and not together.* It is important that children learn to work independently.

C2-5. sim-i-**lar**-i-ty: There is a **similarity** between all good phonics programs because they all teach similar skills such as speech sounds and their spellings.

C2-6. spec-**tac**-u-lar: Students who learn all 936 words in the WISE OWL Polysyllables make spectacular gains in their reading. Their gains in reading are *strikingly large and obvious.*

C2-7. sub-**sid**-i-ar-y: A **subsidiary** is *something less important than, but related to something else*. Some people think handwriting is **subsidiary** to reading, but Mr. Potter says all language skills are equally important. Children need to learn to speak, read, write, and spell well.

C2-8. **tem**-po-rar-i-ly: The lights in the room went off **temporarily** when the storm knocked out the electricity. Temporary means *for a short period of time and not permanently*.

C2-9. trans-**par**-ent: Clear glass is **transparent** because you can *see through it to the object on the other side*.

C2-10. un-fa-**mil**-i-ar: Most first-graders are **unfamiliar** with polysyllables, which is why Mr. Potter wrote this program for them so they can read big words like the big kids. The word **unfamiliar** means *not familiar or unknown*. Un- is a prefix meaning *not*.

C2-11. vo-**cab**-u-lar-y: The bigger your **vocabulary** the better you will read. Rita has a really big **vocabulary** because she learned a lot of *words* in Mr. Potter's WISE OWL Polysyllables program. There are 936 words in the program, but students can read thousands more when they complete the program.

C2-12. **ad**-ver-ti-sing: In **advertising**, people write ads for newspapers and billboards *to let other people know what they have to sell*. I once saw a large billboard along the road **advertising** big juicy hamburgers with a picture of a big juicy hamburger.

C2-13. ar-**rang**e-ment: The WISE OWL Polysyllables are arranged by groups of phonograms. This progressive **arrangement** is the secret of easy polysyllables.

C2-14. **con**-gress-man: A **congressman** is *a person who represents our interests in the legislature.* He helps *make laws* that will help the people who voted him into office.

C2-15. **pen**-e-tra-ting: The raiding party was found **penetrating** the outer defenses of Camelot, but King Arthur and the Knights of the Round Table were able to stop them before they *broke through the walls* of the city. The enemy did not penetrate the walls.

C2-16. pre-**ce**-ding: Raymond Laurita pointed out in a **preceding** article that frustration can cause reading reversals. He talked about it in the article that he published *before* his article on sight-words as a cause of reading problems.

C2-17. rec-**tan**-gu-lar: Lots of objects are shaped like rectangles having four straight sides and four right angles. Can you name some things that are rectangles?

C2-18. **streng**-then: The contractor added lots of steel to the structure of the skyscraper to **strengthen** it enough so it will not fall down in a strong wind. He *made it stronger*.

C2-19. **Wash**-ing-ton: General George **Washington** was a great President. He was a wise and good leader of The United States of America. He was the very first president.

C2-20. ac-**com**-plish: I hope to **accomplish** finishing all of my math homework by bed time this evening. I want to *complete all of it successfully* before I go to bed.

C2-21. as-**ton**-ish-ment: I looked at Annie's beautiful cursive handwriting with **astonishment**. I was *greatly surprised* to see such beautiful handwriting by a third grader.

C2-22. **bat**-tle-ship: A **battleship** is a *large warship with heavy caliber, long range guns and lots of protective armor*. **Battleships** fought many sea battles in World War II.

C2-23. com-**pan**-ion-ship. **Companionship** is *a feeling of friendship*. It is a wonderful thing to know that we have good friends as companions to play with.

Group C3 Wise Owl Polysyllables

C3-1. dic-**ta**-tor-ship: A **dictatorship** is *when a dictator runs a country*. Dictators *are people who have total power and answer to nobody*.

C3-2. es-**tab**-lish-ment: An **establishment** *is an organization or group of people with a purpose*. Mr. Potter would like to establish or start a serious **establishment** to promote phonics.

C3-3. **fash**-ion-a-ble: At one time it was **fashionable** for men to wear wigs. Many men wore hot, itchy white powered wigs for official business. It was a *current popular trend*.

C3-4. **per**-ish-a-ble: You need to be careful with a **perishable** good like milk because it will turn sour if not kept refrigerated. **Perishable** means *something likely to go bad quickly*.

C3-5. **pun**-ish-ment: Everybody knows that crime demands just **punishment**. John had to pay a *penalty* for cheating on his history test. His teacher made him take another history test and his parents did not let him go out with his friends for a whole month. He took his **punishment** and learned his lesson. He does not cheat anymore.

C3-6. **self**-ish-ness: **Selfishness** is not a part of Helen's character. She is not selfish. She is always happy to share her healthy snacks with her classmates. A selfish person *lacks consideration for the needs of others*.

C3-7. de-**ligh**t-ful: Susie is a **delightful** person. She is always *full of happiness and delight*. She is quite charming.

C3-8. flash-l**igh**t: It is good to have a **flashlight** and a fresh supply of batteries nearby in case the electricity goes out during a storm.

C3-9: **straight**-en: Jennifer helped Jeff to **straighten** his tie so it wouldn't be crooked. To **straighten** is *to make straight*.

C3-10. re-**mar**-kȧ-ble: Mr. Rogers is a **remarkable** reading teacher. His method of teaching reading with phonograms is *worthy of attention*. He gets great results.

C3-11. un-mis-**ta**-ka-ble: Mr. Albert Potter's cursive handwriting in **unmistakable**. It would be impossible to mistake it for someone else's cursive. He was a Master Penman.

C3-12. at-**tain**-a-ble: Mr. Potter believes reading well is an **attainable** goal for all children if they are taught intensive phonics. He believes it is an *achievable* goal.

C3-13. a-vail-a-**bil**-i-ty: There is no problem with the **availability** of good children's fountain pens these days at a very reasonable price. They are *available* for purchase from the Internet and local office supply stores.

C3-14. en-ter-**tain**-ment: Mr. Potter plays guitar for **entertainment**. He finds it very *enjoyable* to play Bach's "Chaconne in Dm."

C3-15. **faith**-ful-ly: The Fifth Army followed General Mark Clark **faithfully** into battle because they were loyal to their country and had high regard for their beloved general.

C3-16. **main**-te-nance: Our school has a great **maintenance** person. She makes sure everything is maintained well and in good working order.

C3-17. may-on-**naise**: Did you know that mayonnaise is a *thick, creamy dressing made from egg yolks beaten with oil and vinegar and then seasoned with spices*. Gary likes mayonnaise on his hamburger. He says it makes the hamburger taste real good.

C3-18. mil-lio-**naire**: If Mr. Potter were a **millionaire,** he would use his millions' of dollars to give every first grade teacher in America a copy of <u>Reading Made Easy with Blend Phonics for First Grade</u>. That would be great!

C3-19. **reck**-less-ly: There is no excuse for driving **recklessly**. Reckless people *act without thinking or caring about the consequences of their actions.*

C3-20. **wick**-ed-ness: The **wickedness** of the robbers became clear when they stole candy from a little boy and knocked him down in the mud. Wicked people are *evil*.

C3-21. cir-**cum**-fer-ence: The *distance around something* is its **circumference**. The **circumference** of the Earth is 24,901 miles.

C3-22. **cir**-cum-stance: Jill wanted to ride her bike to school but **circumstances** prevented it. There was a big rain, and she would get soaking wet riding her bike.

C3-23. con-**spir**-a-cy: The **conspiracy** to kill Abraham Lincoln was one of the most famous and dastardly conspiracies in history. John Wilkes Booth conspired with some evil accomplices to assassinate President Lincoln with a derringer at the Ford Theater.

C3-24. **rec**-tan-gle. In contrast to a square, a **rectangle** is *a four-sided figure with four right angles, but adjacent sides are not the same length.* The floor of a basketball court is a **rectangle**.

Group C4 Wise Owl Polysyllables

C4-1. en-**vi**-ron-ment: Jane's fourth-grade class is helping protect the **environment** by recycling plastic drinking bottles. Your **environment** is *the surroundings in which you live.* Everyone deserves a healthy **environment**.

C4-2. ir-**rel**-e-vant: Johnny told the teacher that he couldn't do his math because the lead in his pencil broke. His teacher said that was **irrelevant** because she had just sharpened a dozen pencils for the class. His excuse was *not relevant.* Ir- is another form of the prefix -in.

C4-3. ir-re-**sis**-ti-ble: Joshua said, "Dark chocolate is **irresistible**." It was so delicious that he *could not resist* it. He couldn't turn it down.

C4-4. ir-re-**spon**-si-ble: Harvey fails to do his homework almost everyday. He is **irresponsible**. He is *not responsible* to get his work done.

C4-5. un-de-**sir**-a-ble: Teaching sight-words has the **undesirable** effect of causing some people to develop the whole-word guessing habit. *It is not desirable.*

C4-6. ad-**just**-ment: Little Kenny's seat belt was too tight. His daddy had to make an **adjustment**. An adjustment is *a small change to make something fit or work.*

C4-7. **jus**-ti-fy: Ruby was asked to **justify** her answer on the math quiz. She explained all the steps *to prove she had the right answer.*

C4-8. be-**wil**-der-ment: Rita experienced **bewilderment** when her teacher asked her how to spell "listen." She was *confused* about the silent *t*. She thought it should be spelled *listen*, but her teacher explained the *t* is silent. Listen is the correct spelling.

C4-9. **un**-der-world: Ancient people believed that the dead lived in the **underworld**, which they considered to be somewhere deep in the earth.

C4-10. **worth**-while: Learning to read is very **worthwhile**. It is *worth your time and effort* to learn how to read well.

C4-11. as-**sign**-ment: Mrs. Bailey assigns students pages to read to their parents from Mr. Potter's Blend Phonics Lessons and Stories so her students will have extra opportunity to increase their reading ability. It is their **assignment**.

C4-12. ap-**prox**-i-mate: Kindergarten students should be able to write the alphabet from memory at **approximately** 40 letters per minute. **Approximately** means *more or less*.

C4-13. ex-**as**-per-ate: The students would **exasperate** Mrs. Pearl Monroe when they did not do all their homework assignments. She would get *intensely irritated*.

C4-14. **ex**-cel-lence: **Excellence** in cursive handwriting is what Mr. Albert Potter specialized in. He did an excellent job teaching his students to write excellently. They wrote cursive *very well*.

C4-15. ex-**cite**-ment: You could feel the **excitement** when Annie won the international cursive handwriting competition. She learned with Mr. Potter's Shortcut to Cursive.

C4-16. ex-**clu**-sive-ly: C. S. Lewis, the author of the Chronicles of Narnia, wrote **exclusively** with a dip pen. He used it *to the exclusion of all other kinds* of pens. It was the only kind of pen he used.

C4-17. ex-**or**-bi-tant: There is no need to pay an **exorbitant** price for a fountain pen. *Unreasonably expensive* pens do not write any better than much less expensive fountain pens.

C4-18. ex-**per**-i-ment: Michael Faraday performed an **experiment** that proved that moving a wire in a magnetic field would produce an electric current.

C4-19. ex-**traor**-di-na-ry: Chase is an **extraordinary** motocross racer. He can make jumps nobody else can make. His jumps are *truly remarkable*.

C4-20. flex-i-**bil**-i-ty: Pilates is a good exercise for maintaining **flexibility**. Flexibility is *the ability to bend without breaking*. Mr. Potter has practiced Pilates for over ten years.

C4-21. non-ex-**is**-tent: Dinosaurs are **nonexistent** creatures. They roamed the earth many years ago, but they *do not exist* today.

C4-22. un-ex-**pect**-ed-ly. The electricity went off **unexpectedly** due to the ice storm that broke the electric lines. We were *not expecting* the electricity to go off.

Group C5 Wise Owl Polysyllables

C5-1. **gnaw**-ing: Ruby had a **gnawing** pain in her stomach when she ate too much chocolate at the chocolate party. It was a *persistent distressing* pain.

C5-2. **gnat**: **Gnat** is pronounced /nat/. The letter *g* is not pronounced. A **gnat** is a *little fly that looks something like a mosquito*. Some **gnats** can bite you and some can't.

C5-3. **feigned**: Junior **feigned** sick before school yesterday. He *pretended* he was sick so he would not have to take the history test scheduled yesterday. He was *faking*.

C5-4. **gnash**-ing: Mark started **gnashing** his teeth together when he learned that his mother was not going to let him go to Robert's house to play. He *ground his teeth together*.

C5-5. **gnos**-tic: Fred said he was a **gnostic** when it came to making homemade ice cream. He said he had a *special ancient knowledge* of a secret recipe handed down from Merlin the Magician. Actually it was just a special recipe from his grandmother.

C5-6. con-**sign**-ment: The bookstore agreed to sell Harvey's books about gardening on **consignment**. They agreed to pay Harvey for the books they sold for him.

C5-7. cam-**paign**: Mr. Potter is the founder of the Nationwide Blend Phonics Educational Campaign to restore phonics instruction to all first grade classrooms.

C5-8. be-**nign**: Walter had a fatty tumor on his arm. Fortunately the doctor said it was **benign**. It was *perfectly harmless*.

C5-9. a-**lign**-ment: When Mr. Potter broke his collarbone riding his mountain bike, the doctor used a brace to keep the bones in proper **alignment** so it would heal properly.

C5-10. re-**sign**: It is best not to **resign** from a job until you have another job lined up. Never *leave your job or position* if you do not have another one ready to do.

C5-11. **nur**-ture: Gail knows how to **nurture** her children's love of books by reading great books to them every evening. She just finished reading Cranberry Thanksgiving.

C5-12. **fur**-ther-more: Homer was a great story teller, **furthermore** he was a great singer. His classic adventure books were The Iliad and The Odyssey. **Furthermore** means *also*.

C5-13. re-im-**burse**: Jill promised to **reimburse** Henry for the expenses he incurred fixing her leaking sink. She *repaid* him for his hard work fixing the sink.

C5-14. sur-**vi**-val-ist: Gary took **survivalist** training before he went on a journey in the Amazon Forest. He learned all about *how to survive* alone in the forest.

C5-15. **nurse**-maid: Robert's **nursemaid** had to change his diaper three times. A **nursemaid** is *a woman or girl paid to look after a young child or children*.

C5-16. **tur**-pen-tine: Keith poured **turpentine** on his paint brushes to clean them up to use again. **Turpentine** is an *oil that evaporates quickly that is used in mixing paints*.

C5-17. **tur**-tle: There is a **turtle** in the atrium at Rita's school. The kids like to watch the turtle crawling around in his shell.

C5-18. **af**-ter-burn-er: Military jets have **afterburners** that help them to fly really fast. It is an *extra burner* fitted to the exhaust system of a turbojet to increase thrust.

C5-19. **frank**-fur-ter: My dad loved to eat a **frankfurter**. A **frankfurter** is *seasoned smoke sausage made of beef or pork*. They are good with sauerkraut.

C5-20. **ur**-bà-nite: **Urbanite** rhymes with night. An **urbanite** is *a person who lives in a town or a city*.

C5-21. **cir**-cu-late: June likes to **circulate** at parties. She moves around to be sure that she gets to talk to everybody.

C5-22. af-**firm**-a-tive: Wilson answered in the **affirmative** when asked if he wanted to go mountain climbing with his friends. He *agreed* to go with them. He said, "*Yes*."

C5-23. con-fir-**ma**-tion: Jill got a **confirmation** for her flight from Dallas to Houston. The airline confirmed that her seat was reserved for the flight.

C5-24. **jus**-tice: **Justice** is *what is right and fair*. There is no **justice** in an innocent, little child going hungry. We should all do what that we can to make sure no one suffers from hunger.

Group C6 Wise Owl Polysyllables

C6-1. **fir**-ma-ment: **Firmament** is another word for *sky*. The ancient people spent a lot of time gazing at the stars in the **firmament**.

C6-2. cir-cum-**vent**: The hikers had to **circumvent** a large and dangerous pit in the mountains. They had *to take a path around* it.

C6-3. **work**-shop: Dad had a **workshop** for making fine furniture. He had a *room where he worked* to make chairs, tables, bookshelves, knickknacks, and other things of wood.

C6-4. **fire**-works: Gary loved the **fireworks** on the Fourth of July. He especially liked the rockets filled with gunpowder that would explode way up in the air with a great, dazzling rainbow of colors.

C6-5. **wor**-ship-ful: In church services believers are **worshipful**. They are *full of reverence and worship* as they approach the throne of God with songs and prayers.

C6-6. **worth**-less: Don's new stapler was **worthless**. Every time he tried to staple paper, the staple would get stuck. The stapler was *not worth anything* since it would not staple the paper.

C6-7. **work**-man-ship: Billy's **workmanship** was excellent. He was *skilled at making the best* cabinets and bookshelves.

C6-8. be-**nigh**-ted: The *benighted* children learned to read with phonics. Their world was *like a profoundly dark and starless night* until they learned to read.

C6-9. **work**-a-ble: The students were able to make a **workable** plan for getting homework done. Their plan worked great: homework first, television last.

C6-10. **an**-y-way: Cathy didn't mind when they ran out of ice cream. She didn't want any, **anyway**. Synonyms for *anyway: anyhow, in any case, however, regardless, at any rate*, etc.

C6-11. **high**-way: We took the *main road*, Highway 191, to Midland because the **highway** is faster than the country road.

C6-12. **day**-light: **Daylight** is the *bright light of the sun during the day*. Nightlight, on the other hand, is the dim light of the moon and stars at night.

C6-13. **wor**-ry: Jimmy had a real reason to **worry** about his spelling test. He was *anxious and uneasy* about it because he had failed to study the words.

C6-14. **prayer**-ful-ly: I will **prayerfully** consider your job offer. I will *pray about it a lot*.

C6-15. **main**-stay: The fast, highflying SR-71 Blackbird spy plane was the **mainstay** of America's spy program for many years. It was the *main* aerial surveillance vehicle.

C6-16. dis-**may**: Mary felt **dismay** when she failed the practice spelling test on Monday, but her *feeling of distress* vanished when she got an A+ on Friday's test.

C6-17. **drive**-way: You can park your car in the **driveway**. The **driveway** is a *short road from a public road to a house or garage*.

C6-18. **pay**-a-ble: Mary bought her son a new mountain bike. She made the check **payable** to Mountain Bikes Etc. Mountain Bikes Etc. cashed the check and *got the money*.

C6-19. **could**-n't: **Couldn't** is a contraction for *could not*. Marcia **couldn't** keep from laughing at the funny story.

C6-20: **would**-n't: David **wouldn't** eat spinach until he watched Popeye, and saw how strong it made him. He *would not* eat it until he saw the cartoon.

C6-21. **should**-n't: You **shouldn't** eat too much chocolate at one time. You *should not* eat it because it can make you sick.

C6-22. **news**-pa-per: Uncle Bob reads the **newspaper** everyday. The **newspaper** is basically *a lot of unstapled sheets of paper printed on both sides with lots of news and advertising*.

C6-23. **dew**-drop: Some people say you can see the whole world in a single **dewdrop** if you look close enough. Dew is the water you see on leaves early in the morning.

C6-24. re-**view**: Mr. Potter has written a **review** of Mrs. Dolores Hisks' book *Phonics Pathways*. He taught the book and wrote an article on Amazon about how great it was.

C6-25. **jew**-el-ry: Fine **jewelry** like necklaces and rings contain beautiful gems that often cost a lot of money.

C6-26. **mil**-dew: Mom uses bleach to keep **mildew** from growing on the shower wall. Mildew is a *white powdery mold* that can grow on damp surfaces.

C6-27. re-**new**-al: My guitar magazine sent me a notice that it was time for **renewal** of my subscription. I sent them the money *to renew my subscription* so I can keep getting the magazine every month.

C6-28. re-**view**-er: A **reviewer** is *a person who reads a book or article and makes any suggestions necessary to make it better*. Mr. Potter has reviewed several books for writers.

C6-29. **strewn**: Professor Elliott's books were **strewn** all over the place. They were *untidily scattered* around the room. He was sorting through all his books to see what he could donate to the public library.

C6-30. **par**-a-llel: The teacher asked Henry to draw **parallel** lines in geometry class using a protractor and ruler. The *lines were side by side and went on like that forever without ever touching.*

Group D Symbol-to-Sound Relationships

z aw au kn wr oi oy
ph oa qu ui eigh dge tion

Group D1 Wise Owl Polysyllables

D1-1. **cap**-i-tal-ize: There are two main kinds of letters: uppercase and lowercase. The *uppercase* letters are also called capital letters. **Capitalize** is *a verb meaning to use uppercase or capital letters*:
ABCDEFGHIJKLMNOPQRSTUVWXYZ.

D1-2. **cen**-tral-ize: Socialist governments believe we should **centralize** the control of every aspect of society in the hands of the government. It has never worked.

D1-3. **cit**-i-zen-ship: Jose was proud when he got his United States **citizenship**. He passed all the *legal requirements to become a full citizen* of the United States.

D1-4. com-**pu**-ter-ized: Mr. Potter believes that no **computerized** system for teaching reading will ever be better than his trusty old fashioned chalkboard and time tested linguistic phonics program. He always gets superior results teaching from his trusty old chalkboard.

D1-5. **fer**-ti-li-zer: **Fertilizer** is a *substance added to the soil to make plants grow better*. It is *food for plants*. Your yard will be greener if you fertilize it with grass **fertilizer**.

D1-6. ho-ri-**zon**-tal: Sarah is great on the **horizontal** bars in gymnastics. The bars are *parallel to the ground.*

D1-7. **sym**-pa-thize: Devin can **sympathize** with people who were not taught to read with phonics. He knows *how they feel* because he could not read till Mr. Potter taught him phonics.

D1-8. **straw**-ber-ry: There is nothing better than **strawberry** on ice cream or oatmeal. Do you like strawberries on your cereal or ice cream?

D1-9. ab-bre-vi-**a**-tion: An **abbreviation** is *a short form of a word or phrase* that can save you lots of space when you write. DOD stands for Department of Defense. Mr. stands for mister. B. A. stands for Bachelor of Arts degree.

D1-10. ac-cum-u-**la**-tion: Marty has a large **accumulation** of excellent books. He has been *gathering them for a long time.* They cover many excellent subjects that help him to be smarter.

D1-11. ac-cu-**sa**-tion: The teacher made an unwarranted **accusation** against Johnny last Friday. She *accused* him of cheating on his spelling test. She apologized when he spelled all the words to her correctly on a retake.

D1-12. ad-**di**-tion-al: Mrs. Monroe let Karen do **additional** work to bring up her grades. Mrs. Monroe *added extra work* that Karen could do to raise her grade average.

D1-13. ad-min-is-**tra**-tion: Every school district needs a good **administration**. The **administration** consists of the *people who administer education under an executive officer*. They hire and train teachers, choose curriculum, and are responsible to see that all students get a good education.

D1-14. ad-mi-**ra**-tion: Mr. Donald Potter has a lot of **admiration** for the brave teachers who taught phonics when it was not popular. He *admires and thinks highly* of them.

D1-15. co-**in**-ci-dence: It is no **coincidence** that students who learn to read and spell with phonics are better readers and spellers than those who are taught with sight-words. It did not *happen by accident without any causal relationship*.

D1-16. àf-**fec**-tion-àte: Mary was *affectionate* toward her new baby. She *loved her a lot*. Young children need a lot of love if they are to grow up to be healthy and happy.

D1-17. àf-**flic**-tion: Junior had an **affliction** of the nervous system that caused him *to suffer* with anxiety and worry all the time. He overcame it by meditating daily on Psalms 23.

D1-18. am-mu-**ni**-tion: The Supply Officer was in charge of making sure that the brave soldiers had enough **ammunition**. They needed enough *bullets* so they would never run out of ammunition during a long battle.

D1-19. ap-pli-**ca**-tion: The **application** of sun screen is important if you plan to spend a lot of time in the direct sunlight. You should *apply it* liberally and frequently to protect yourself from a bad sunburn. **Application** can also be *a form you fill out to apply for a job*.

D1-20. as-sas-si-**na**-tion: The **assassination** of President Abraham Lincoln was a real blow to an honorable and successful reconstruction of the South. John Wilkes Booth *assassinated* President Lincoln on April 14, 1865.

D1-21. as-**sump**-tion: That manuscript handwriting is better than cursive handwriting for beginning writers is a common **assumption** that is easily proven false. It is *assumed true without proof*.

D1-22. cal-cu-**la**-tion: **Calculation** *determines the size or number of something*. Teachers use a simple formula to calculate students' grades.

D1-24: re-**demp**-tion. Redemption is *the act of regaining something in exchange for payment*. Rodger was able to redeem his guitar from the pawnshop by buying it back.

D1-25: **sta**-tion: The call sign of Mr. Potter's amateur radio **station** is NG5W. He can talk to people around the world with voice or Morse Code.

Group D2 Wise Owl Polysyllables

D2-1. cir-cu-**la**-tion: William Harvey was the Englishman who discovered the **circulation** of blood in the human body. He discovered that blood *flowed around and around* in the human body due to the pumping action of the heart.

D2-2. civ-i-li-**za**-tion: Western **Civilization** was greatly influenced by Greek philosophy, Roman law, and the Christian religion. Civilization is *our institutions and way of life*.

D2-3. com-pli-**ca**-tion: I started to build a spaceship once, but ran into a **complication**. Building a spaceship far too *complicated and difficult* for a ten year old!

D2-4. con-sti-**tu**-tion: A **constitution** is *a body of fundamental principles or established precedents according to which a state or other organization is acknowledged to be governed*. How did you like that definition? Our **Constitution** is the *law of the land*.

D2-5. con-**struc**-tion: Junior Williams worked on a big **construction** project that built the Markland Dam across the Ohio River near Madison, Indiana.

D2-6. con-tra-**dic**-tion: The good cursive handwriting of Mr. Potter's kindergarten students is a **contradiction** of the common opinion that kindergarten students cannot learn cursive. A contradiction is *something that is the opposite*. They all learned his Shortcut to Cursive.

D2-7. cor-po-**ra**-tion: The word **corporation** comes from a Latin word meaning "combine in one body." It is *a company or group of people authorized to act as a single entity and recognized as such in law*. Ford Motor Company is a very large **corporation**.

D2-8. des-**crip**-tion: Annie's cursive handwriting is beautiful beyond **description**. It *looks like* it was written by a highly skilled calligrapher.

D2-9. des-ti-**na**-tion: Our **destination** for summer vacation was Bremen, Indiana. We were *going there to spend some time* with our family on a beautiful grain farm.

D2-10. **dic**-tion-ar-y: The main tool for expanding your vocabulary is a good **dictionary**. Your dictionary *lists words in alphabetical order and gives you the pronunciation, meaning, and usage of every word*. Mr. Potter used his dictionary often when writing <u>WISE OWL Polysyllables</u>.

D2-11. e-**val**-u-a-tion: Chase did an **evaluation** of his new motocross bike. He rode it for a long time on some very difficult trails *to evaluate how well it would preform* in a race.

D2-12. ex-am-i-**na**-tion: Mr. Potter had to pass a difficult **examination** to be a Spanish teacher. The *test* examined his ability to understand, read, speak, and write Spanish.

D2-13. ex-hi-**bi**-tion: An **exhibition** is *a public display of a work of art or other item of interest*. Mr. Macintyre's students like to exhibit their cursive handwriting and 3-D pictures on the walls outside their classroom.

D2-14. ex-pla-**na**-tion: Dorothea gave an excellent **explanation** of the principals of rocket propulsion to her science class. She *explained* the principles of propulsion.

D2-15. **func**-tion-al: Mr. O'Neal took a **functional** approach to teaching English grammar. He showed how knowing the functions of the parts of speech in sentences could help his students communicate better in English.

D2-16. hu-mil-i-**a**-tion: The Buffalo Juniors were **humiliated** when they lost their first basketball game of the season. They *felt ashamed* that they lost the game.

D2-17. i-den-ti-fi-**ca**-tion: They verified Orson's **identification** at the airport by checking the picture and name on his driver's license. They made sure it was actually him.

D2-18. in-di-**ca**-tion: Judy's good grades this six weeks are a good **indication** that she is making progress. It is a *sign* that she has been studying and learning.

D2-19. in-for-**ma**-tion: Reading tests give Mr. Potter the **information** he needs to know how to help kids read better. The tests give him the *facts* he needs to know.

D2-20. in-**spec**-tion: Before taking off in his airplane, James makes a complete visual **inspection**. He makes a *careful examination* of all the exterior and moving parts.

D2-21. in-**struc**-tion: Mrs. Collins is an expert in elementary school **instruction**. She can *teach* cursive handwriting, grammar, history, arithmetic, spelling, geography, English and all the other subjects they need to know.

D2-22. in-**ten**-tion-al-ly: To do something **intentionally** is *to do it deliberately or on purpose*. Rodger did not **intentionally** mean to run over his Mom's flowers. It was an accident.

D2-23. in-ter-**na**-tion-al: The nations of South America made an **international** treaty not to engage in war with each other. It was a treaty *between all the nations*.

D2-24. jus-ti-fi-**ca**-tion: There was no **justification** for Bonnie telling Sally that she was ugly. There was no reason for it. Her dad made her apologize, and she did.

D2-25: con-**di**-tion: Before buying a used car, Dad always has Grandpa Bob take it for a test drive to make sure it is in good **condition**. Grandpa Bob knows all about cars.

Group D3 Wise Owl Polysyllables

D3-1. in-ter-**rup**-tion: There was an **interruption** of the television program for a newsflash that a bad storm was coming. They *stopped* the program to give the weather.

D3-2. in-tro-**duc**-tion: The **introduction** of the steam engine lead to great advances in transportation, including steam powered ships, trains, and even cars.

D3-3. in-vi-**ta**-tion: Harold sent Kathleen an invitation to his birthday party. He *invited* her to celebrate with him.

D3-4. lim-i-**ta**-tion: Mr. Maltz says there is no **limitation** to the human imagination. He believes that any person can achieve what he or she can imagine.

D3-5. mal-**func**-tion: The water cooler at school had a **malfunction** today. It *didn't work right*. The water was too hot to drink.

D3-6. mis-con-**cep**-tion: There is a *misconception* about teaching phonics. Some say it is boring, but Mr. Potter's students say it is fun. Some have an *incorrect opinion*.

D3-7. mul-ti-pli-**ca**-tion: It is very important to learn the **multiplication** table if you plan to make good grades at arithmetic. Multiplication is just *a quick way to count equal groups of things*.

D3-9. pop-u-**la**-tion: The population of our city is 90,000. That many people live in our city. The population refers to *all the inhabitants in a particular town, area, or county*.

D3-10. pro-nun-ci-**a**-tion: Use the respelling in the dictionary to learn the **pronunciation** of any word you have never heard before. **Pronunciation** is *the way words are pronounced*.

D3-11. pro-**tec**-tion: Motocross racers wear safety gear for the **protection** of their bodies in a crash. A good helmet can save a life by protecting your head.

D3-12. pub-li-**ca**-tion: Mr. Potter was looking forward to the **publication** of WISE OWL Polysyllables. He thanks you for purchasing this copy and trusts that your reading is improving a lot.

D3-13. re-dis-tri-**bu**-tion: **Redistribution** just *means to distribute again*, like passing out papers again.

D3-14. re-ha-**bil**-i-ta-tion: After the bad car accident, Mary had to go through **rehabilitation** to learn to walk again. To rehabilitate is *to restore to health*.

D3-15. re-**cep**-tion: The news that school was going to be ten days longer this year did not meet with a good **reception**. The children *did not receive* the idea very well.

D3-16. re-pro-**duc**-tion: I saw a full size **reproduction** of Christopher Columbus' Santa Maria that is *just like the original*. They actually sailed it across the Atlantic.

D3-17. rep-u-**ta**-tion: People of good repute have a good **reputation**. They live good and helpful lives so they earn a good reputation. Henry has a **reputation** for being an honest car salesman. He always tells the truth about his cars.

D3-18. res-er-**va**-tion: Tom made a **reservation** for a flight to Indianapolis, Indiana to see his mother. The airlines *saved him a seat* for the flight.

D3-19. sub-**scrip**-tion: Mr. Greenwood has a **subscription** for an amateur radio magazine that he receives each month. He *pays a year ahead to get the magazine each month*.

D3-20. tra-**di**-tion-al: Mr. Potter is a **traditional** teacher. He teaches phonics reading and cursive handwriting from a chalkboard. He is old fashioned and effective.

D3-21. au-di-**tor**-i-um: All the children sat quietly in the **auditorium** during the music concert. An **auditorium** is *the part of a building where an audience sits to listen*.

D3-22. au-to-**mat**-i-cal-ly: The automatic car wash **automatically** washes the car. It does all the work so the driver just sits and waits in the car till the wash is finished.

D3-23. au-to-mo-**bil**e: The word **automobile** comes from the French words **auto** (self) and **mobile** (move). It is a car that has a motor and *moves by itself.*

D3-24. sal-**va**-tion: **Salvation** is the *Christian teaching that Jesus saves people from their sins.* They believe that He makes them right with God through faith in His blood.

D3-24. in-car-**na**-tion: The **incarnation** is the Christian teaching that *God became a man by means of a miraculous birth* in order to save men from their sins.

D3-25. cer-ti-fi-**ca**-tion. Mr. Potter has his **certification** as a bilingual teacher. He has an *official document* from the State of Texas *that proves that he is certified* by the State.

D3-26: pro-cla-**ma**-tion: Abraham Lincoln issued the Emancipation **Proclamation** on January 2, 1863 that freed all the slaves in the ten states in rebellion.

Group D4 Wise Owl Polysyllables

D4-1. **res**-tau-rant: What is your favorite **restaurant**? Susie says her favorite restaurant is Manual's Mexican **Restaurant**. She likes tacos and burritos every morning for breakfast.

D4-2. ap-**point**-ment: I need to make an **appointment** to get new brakes on my Tundra pickup truck. An appointment is *an arrangement to meet someone at a particular time and place.*

D4-3. dis-ap-**point**-ment: Rafael felt **disappointment** when he did not make the basketball team. He *felt sad because he did not get to play.*

D4-4. at-mos-**phere**: The weatherman said that there was a disturbance in the **atmosphere** that was causing us to have so much rain. The **atmosphere** consists of *the gases surrounding the earth.* Nitrogen and oxygen are the two main gases in our **atmosphere**.

D4-5. ca-**tas**-tro-phe: A **catastrophe** is a *terrible disaster*. Judy missed all the words on her pretest in spelling. She said it was a disaster. But she got all the words right on the Friday test, thanks to Mrs. Pate's tutoring.

D4-6. diph-**ther**-i-a: **Diphtheria** is a *disease caused by a harmful bacteria* that used to make a lot of people very sick before scientists discovered a vaccine that prevented it.

D4-7. em-**phat**-i-cal-ly: To speak **emphatically** is *to speak in a forceful way.* Jessie **emphatically** claimed his dog ate his homework. He had a cell phone picture to prove it!

D4-8. **hem**-is-phere: A *hemisphere* is *half a sphere.* Judy's teacher told her that the United States is in the northern **hemisphere** on the globe of the Earth.

D4-9. so-**phis**-ti-ca-ted: Cars these days are very **sophisticated** machines. They have been *developed to a high degree of complexity.* Years ago cars were much simpler since they had fewer parts and few electronic devices.

D4-10. tri-**um**-phant-ly: Andrew *triumphantly* told his grandpa Potter that he had finished reading all the stories in Blend Phonics Lessons and Stories. Andrew was very happy that he had read the whole book by himself. They celebrated with a delicious pizza!

D4-11. **black**-board: Andrew drew a picture of a destructive volcano on the **blackboard** in grandpa Don's classroom. He used chalk to draw and label the pictures. Great job Andrew! Keep up the good work.

D4-12. ac-**quain**-tance: Junior was just an **acquaintance** of mine. I *knew a little* about him, but he was *not a close friend*.

D4-13. **ad**-e-quate-ly: Rudy had not prepared himself **adequately** for his test on the Revolutionary War. His preparation was not *sufficient* to get a high grade.

D4-14. **con**-se-quence: As a **consequence** of forgetting to fill the helium balloons for Jill's birthday party, we ended up having the party without the balloons. **Consequence** means *the results of an action or condition*.

D4-15. e-**quiv**-a-lent: Homer bought four quart cartons of milk. He could have just bought one-gallon jug of milk since one gallon is **equivalent** to four quarts. They are *equal in amount*.

D4-16. **fre**-quent-ly: Andrew **frequently** rides his mountain bike with Grandpa Potter. They *often* ride at the Permian Basin Mountain Bike Park in Odessa, TX.

D4-17. in-**ad**-e-quate: Judy's preparation for the physics test was **inadequate**. It *was not adequate or sufficient* to pass the test. Fortunately she passed the final test and brought up her average grade.

D4-18. mas-quer-**ade**: Penny had a **masquerade** party at her house last week. Everybody dressed up in pirate *disguises*.

D4-19. qual-i-fi-**ca**-tion: One **qualification** for becoming an Air Force pilot is good vision. Good vision is one of the things that make a person *qualified to* fly a military airplane.

D4-20. ques-tion-**naire**: The doctor usually has new patients fill out a **questionnaire** concerning any health problems. A **questionnaire** is *a written list of questions to answer*.

D4-21. re-**quire**-ment: Cursive is a **requirement** at the school where Mr. Potter teaches. Everyone is *required* to learn cursive and use it for all their writing assignments.

D4-22. in-**fre**-quent-ly: Infrequent means *not frequent*. The prefix **–in** means *not*. **Frequent** means *often*. So **Infrequent** means *not often*. **–ly** makes it an adverb.

D4-23. **sui**-ta-bil-i-ty: **Suitability** is a noun that means *right or appropriate for a particular person or situation*. It is important to check the **suitability** of a bicycle for a child to make sure it is the right size for that child.

D4-24. star-**va**-tion: Mary's puppy almost died of **starvation** when he got lost in the woods. He couldn't find any food. Mary finally found him and nursed him back to health. **Starvation** is *suffering or death caused by hunger*.

D4-25. sanc-ti-fi-**ca**-tion: **Sanctification** is *the process of declaring something holy or special*. The Gettysburg battlefield is said to be sanctified by the blood of the brave soldiers who died there.

D4-26. mo-ti-**va**-tion. Chase had a lot of **motivation** to win the Annual Motocross Race in Anaheim, California last year. He *really wanted to win* the big trophy.

Group D5 Wise Owl Polysyllables

D5-1. **noise**-less-ly: Hobbits can move **noiselessly** through the forest. Bilbo Baggins was a famous Hobbit who could walk through the forest *without making a sound*. He was very stealthy.

D5-2: re-**size**: To **resize** is *to alter or change the size of something*. Mr. Potter sometimes has to **resize** the window on the screen of his computer.

D5-3. **choice**-es: Martha had several **choices** of colleges when she graduated from high school. She was accepted at MIT, Harvard, Yale, and UCLA. She chose to go to Yale because that's where her mom and dad went.

D5-4. **fro**-zen: A Popsicle is a delicious **frozen** treat. **Frozen** is the past tense of freeze. To freeze *means to turn a liquid to a solid by lowering the temperature*.

D5-5. **joint**-ed: A joint is where two things come together such as the joints in our fingers. Some people are double **jointed** and can bend their fingers way back.

D5-6. **zest**-ful-ly: June lives **zestfully**. She is *full of zest and enthusiasm*. Today she is *zestfully* filling boxes with candy to send to soldiers in the Armed Forces.

D5-7. **poin**-ter: Mr. Jones uses a **pointer** to point to the phonograms and words on the chalkboard. **Pointers** are great since they help students pay attention to what is important. It helps them get the point!

D5-8. **zip**-per: Many clothes these days have **zippers**. **Zippers** are especially nice for children who find that it is hard to use buttons or tie shoestrings.

D5-9. ex-ploi-**ta**-tion: The Spanish Conquistadores **exploitation** of the Native Americans was terrible. They *treated them unfairly* by making them work long hard hours in deep, dark, dangerous gold mines without any pay and kept all the gold for themselves.

D5-10. **cra**-zy: Mr. Potter is **crazy** about dark chocolate. He *likes it a lot*. What are you crazy about?

D5-11. **oint**-ment: The doctor gave Judy a special **ointment** to put on her hands to clear up an itchy rash. It was *smooth oil* that had healing medicine in it.

D5-12. **puz**-zle-ment: My Potter feels a lot of **puzzlement** as to why everyone doesn't teach reading with phonics. He is *puzzled* and *confused* about the lack of good phonics. <u>Reading Made Easy with Blend Phonics for First Grade</u> is a good program.

D5-13. a-**void**-a-ble: The wreck was **avoidable**. It *didn't have to happen*. It *could have been avoided*. City planners should do all they can to make the city streets safe for traffic.

D5-14. **ze**-ro: Harry got a **zero** on his spelling paper. He missed every spelling word. He got *nothing*. Fortunately his teacher gave him a second chance, and he got them all correct, with a little help from Mr. Santos.

D5-16. **bap**-tize: **Baptize** is an English word that comes from the Greek language. It originally meant to *immerse*. Ancient Greek writers used it of *immersing* all kinds of things, including sinking ships.

D5-17. **an**-a-lyze: To **analyze** is *to study or examine something carefully*. Mr. Potter likes to **analyze** sentences to determine all the parts of speech. There are eight parts of speech: nouns, pronouns, adjectives, verbs, adverbs, conjunctions, prepositions, and interjections.

D5-18. de-**stroy**-er: The navy has many **destroyers**. A destroyer is a *small, fast warship used to defend a fleet against enemy submarines and aircraft*.

D5-19. **mem**-or-ize: Lewis loved to **memorize** passages from Shakespeare's plays. He l*earned them by heart by committing them to memory*. His favorite quote is from Hamlet, "This above all: to thine own self be true."

D5-20. un-em-**ploy**-ment: Junior is **unemployed**. He has looked everywhere for a job but can't find work anywhere. He is *not employed*.

D5-21. ad-**di**-tion-al: Junior asked his teacher for **additional** work to bring up his history grade. He wanted to do some *extra* work to get some extra credit.

D5-22. di-**rec**-tion: Ransom told Bob that he was going in the wrong **direction**. He turned left when he should have turned right.

D5-23. in-**ten**-tion-al: Anything that is **intentional** is *done on purpose*. Judy did not intentionally knock over Ruby's lemonade stand. She accidentally knocked it over.

Group D6 Wise Owl Polysyllables

D6-1. **re**-a-lize: When Balser Brent was able to **realize** there was a huge black bear in the path, he quickly aimed his trusty smooth bore carbine rifle and shot the bear through the heart. He was a brave hunter. For the details, read *The Bears of Blue River* by Charles Major.

D6-2. re-a-li-**za**-tion: The **realization** that there was a fierce black bear in the path caused Balser to act fast to save his life. **Realization** is *the act of becoming fully aware of something as a fact.*

D6-3. an-**noy**-ance: Julie's constant tapping of her pencil on her desk was an **annoyance** to everybody in the class. They were *irritated* with her annoying tapping. Her teacher solved the problem by giving her a fountain pen!

D6-4. **toy**-ing: Jimmy was **toying** with the idea of making a model rocket. He was *considering the idea casually*. He was not really serious about it because he knew he might get hurt.

D6-5: **ci**-ti-zen-ship: The Apostle Paul had Roman **citizenship**. He was *legally recognized as a citizen* of the Roman Empire. It saved his life once. You can read about in the Book of Acts by Luke the Physician.

D6-6. **joy**-ful-ly: Mrs. Pearl Monroe **joyfully** taught us all how to read in first grade with phonics. She was *full of joy* when she saw us reading our textbooks.

D6-7. **hyp**-no-tize: Professor William James wrote a whole chapter about hypnosis in his famous *Principles of Psychology*. Hypnotized people are said to be *under the control of the hypnotist*.

D6-8. **vis**-ua-lize: It will help you to read better if you can **visualize** the scenes in the stories. To visualize is *to form a mental image or picture*. It helps to have a good imagination.

D6-9. **nat**-ur-a-lize: When a person from a foreign country *becomes a citizen of another country*, they are said to be **naturalized.** Albert Einstein was born in Germany, but he was naturalized and became an American citizen.

D6-10. **au**-di-o: Mr. Richardson has made lots of **audio** recordings for his students to help them learn to read better. The word **audio** *means sounds, especially speech sounds*.

D6-11. **knight**-hood: The brave knights believed in **knighthood**. They faithfully served their lord and fought to save the lovely princess. They believed in chivalry.

D6-12. au-**xil**-ia-ry: Mr. Shugar was Mr. Potter's **auxiliary**. He *helped* Mr. Potter teach bilingual children to read and write English and Spanish. He was a great help.

D6-13. **knife**: George has a Buck pocket **knife**. **Knife** is not a polysyllable, but it is presented here to teach the phonogram kn- that has the /n/ sound.

D6-14. au-**then**-tic: There is an **authentic** copy of the Declaration of Independent in Washington, DC. It is an *undisputedly genuine* copy.

D6-15. **kneel**-ing: The Apostle Paul could often be seen **kneeling** to pray. He believed that God could hear and answer his prayers. He kneeled to *show honor* to God.

D6-16. **au**-thor-ize: The School Board **authorized** the Principal to buy chalkboards for all the classrooms. They gave *official approval* for the purchase.

D6-17. **knap**-sack: Billy carried his **knapsack** on the long march through the forest. It was *a strong, waterproof bag with shoulder straps* to make it easier to carry.

D6-18. **knack**: Orson had the **knack** of making people laugh and feel good. It was a *natural skill* of his. He knew lots of funny jokes.

D6-19. **knuck**-le: Kim hurt the **knuckles** of her right hand when she fell off her bike the other day. The letter *k* in **knuckles** is silent; don't say it, but be sure to write it.

D6-20. **ac**-tion: There was a lot of **action** on the basketball court today. The team got on the move and made ten baskets to win the game.

D6-21. cog-**ni**-tion: Here is a word you don't see everyday. **Cognition** is *the mental action or process of acquiring knowledge through thought, experience, and the senses*. In everyday language it just means *thinking*. Have you experienced any **cognition** today?

D6-22. no-ti-fi-**ca**-tion: The library sent Ron a **notification** that his library book was overdue. They notified him with an email.

Group D7 Wise Owl Polysyllables

D7-1. **wri**-ter: J. R. Tolkein was a great **writer**. He wrote one of Mr. Potter's favorite books: The Hobbit. *Anyone who writes* is a **writer**. I hope you write a good story someday.

D7-2. **writ**-ten: Have you **written** any stories, yet? **Written** is the *past participle of to write*. Mr. Potter has **written** several poems about education.

D7-3. **wrote**: Robert Frost **wrote** many great poems about country life in New England. Mr. Potter's favorite poem by Robert Frost is, "A Time to Talk." He hopes you read it.

D7-4. **straw**-ber-ry: **Strawberries** taste good on oatmeal in the morning with a touch of honey and handful of walnuts. **Strawberries** are *sweet soft red fruit with seeds on the surface*.

D7-5. **wretch**-ed: A **wretched** person is *someone who is very unhappy or unfortunate.* Susie felt very **wretched** after walking all the way home in the pouring rain. Her brand new school dress was soaking wet.

D7-6. **draw**-bridge: The brave knights entered the castle over the **drawbridge**, which could be drawn up to deny their enemy access to the castle.

D7-7. **wrin**-kle: Mom always ironed the **wrinkles** out of our shirts and pants. A **wrinkle** is *a slight line or fold in a fabric.*

D7-8. **flaw**-less-ly: Julie read Robert Frost's Poem, "Time to Talk" *flawlessly.* She *did not make a single mistake.* It is a great a poem. You should read it sometime.

D7-9. **hand**-wri-ting: **Handwriting** is one of Mr. Potter's favorite subjects to teach, especially cursive. Three of his girl students won an international cursive handwriting contest in 2015, and he won Outstanding Teacher of the Year. Thanks girls!

D7-10. **yawn**-ing: Donald was **yawning** because his algebra teacher was boring. She could make any subject boring.

D7-11. **type**-wri-ter: Mr. Potter still has his Royal Safari Portable **Typewriter**. A **typewriter** is *a machine that prints letters and characters when you push keys with your fingers.*

D7-12. **lawn**-mow-er: Mr. Bailey bought an electric **lawnmower**. He uses it *to cut the grass* in his yard. He likes it because it is quiet and requires little maintenance.

D7-13. **ship**-wreck: The sinking of the Titanic was the most tragic **shipwreck** in history. **Shipwreck** is a compound word from ship + wreck.

D7-14. **fawn**-ing-ly: **Fawningly** *means to display exaggerated flattery or affection.* Mr. Elliott went to a Beatles rock concert at Cincinnati Gardens one time. The fans were screaming and yelling **fawningly** at the stars. They displayed *exaggerated affection.*

D7-15. **awk**-ward-ly: Many students hold their pencils **awkwardly**, like a mechanic holding a screwdriver. Mr. Potter teaches them to write better by holding their pencils correctly with a tripod grip. A proper grip makes it easy and enjoyable to write stress free for hours on end.

D7-16. **Sphinx**: The **Sphinx** is *a mysterious ancient stone figure having a lion's body and a human or animal head.* It stands near the Pyramids at Giza.

D7-17. **launch**-er: A **launcher** is *a structure that holds a rocket during launch.* It holds the rocket in an upright position so it doesn't fall over during the launch.

D7-18: **neph**-ew: A **nephew** is *the son of one's brother or sister, or of one's brother-in-law or sister-in-law.* Mr. Palmer has two **nephews** on his side of the family.

D7-19: **fraud**-u-lent: **Fraudulent** is *when a person tricks or deceives someone in order to get what they want.* Mack was guilty of **fraudulent** behavior when he lied about his age to ride the tilt-a-wheel at the fair.

D7-20: **pho**-ton: The word **photon** comes from the Greek word for *light*. Any English word that uses the letters ph to represent the /f/ sound is from the Greek language. It is a Greek phonogram. A **photon** is *a particle of light.*

D7-22. **phys**-i-cal: Kenny is in great **physical** and mental shape. He is in good shape in *body* and mind. He can run for miles and do lots of calisthenics without tiring.

Group D8 Wise Owl Polysyllables

D8-1. au-to-**ma**-tic: Reading words is a skill that should be **automatic**. Fluent readers are able to identify most words *automatically without conscious thought.*

D8-2: **dol**-phins: **Dolphins** are *small toothed whales* that are well known for their sociable nature and high intelligence.

D8-3. **haun**-ted: Jacob went to a **haunted** house with Mr. Jefferson on Halloween. Jacob asked Mr. Jefferson if the house was really haunted. Mr. Jefferson replied, "I hope not!"

D8-4. phy-**si**-cian: Dr. Conrad was a great **physician**. He was *qualified to practice medicine* and help sick people get well. Physicians learn medicine in college.

D8-5. ex-**haust**-ing: Mountain climbing is **exhausting** work. It will *make you very tired*. Tenzing Norgay and Edmund Hillary were officially the first to climb Mount Everest, the tallest mountain in the world.

D8-6. **phys**-ics: Mr. Huron was Mr. Potter's **physics** teacher. He taught Donald about *matter and energy*. Mr. Huron was one of Mr. Potter's favorite teachers.

D8-7. **con**-se-quent-ly: **Consequently** is an adverb meaning *as a result*. Sarah studied hard; **consequently**, she got an A+ on her difficult history test on the Civil War.

D8-8. al-pha-**be**-ti-cal: One of the first things a first grader should learn is how to put words in *ABC order*. As soon as Rodger learned **alphabetical** order, he was able to use his children's dictionary to learn new words by himself.

D8-9. **juic**-i-est: Marge said that Florida grows the juiciest oranges. She said they are *full of sweet juice*.

D8-10. em-**pha**-tic: Frodo, the Hobbit, was **emphatic** when he said, "I will take the Ring, though I do not know the way." Elrond gave an **emphatic** response, "I think this task is appointed for you Frodo; and that if you do not find a way, no one will." Both *spoke forcefully and clearly*.

D8-11. **cruis**-ing: Harold and Rose went **cruising** in the Bahamas. They took a summer *vacation on a ship to visit several ports* in the Bahamas.

D8-12. **sym**-pho-ny: Mr. Potter's favorite **symphony** is Joaquin Rodriguez' "Concerto de Aranjuez." It features a guitar and full orchestra. It is a very beautiful composition.

D8-13. **fruit**-ful: Jerry's apple tree was very **fruitful**. It *produced a lot of fruit*.

D8-14. **pho**-bi-a: Kerry had a **phobia** called claustrophobia. A **phobia** is *an irrational fear that has no basis in fact*. He was *afraid* of confined places.

D8-15. pur-**suit**: Corporal Dayton was in hot **pursuit** of a bank robber. He *chased* him till he caught him and brought him to justice. Corporal Dayton always gets his man!

D8-16. **par**-a-graph: Mr. Potter's favorite Bible is the Cambridge Paragraphed King James Bible. It is written in **paragraphs** like a modern book, instead of versus. A **paragraph** is a *short piece of writing that has one main idea and is indicated by a new line, indentation or numbering*.

D8-17. **law**-suit: The brilliant Nicoli Telsa was involved in a **lawsuit** over one of his patents. It was about one of his great inventions involving alternating current. His lawyer filed a **lawsuit** to keep Thomas Edison from stealing his patent.

D8-18. am-**phi**-bi-an: A frog is an **amphibian** because it lives part of its younger life in the water and its adult life on land. The Army has amphibious vehicles that can travel on both land and water.

D8-19: **suit**-case: A **suitcase** comes in handy when you travel. It *is a case with a handle and hinges used for carrying clothes and other personal items.*

D8-20. phi-**los**-o-phy: **Philosophy** is a word from the Greek language meaning *"the love of wisdom."* Socrates, Plato, and Aristotle are well known ancient Greek philosophers.

D8-21. **suit**-a-ble: It is important to make sure your bicycle is **suitable** for you. It has to be just the *right size for you* to ride comfortably and safely.

D8-22. **soar**-ing: The pretty robin was **soaring** through the air. It was *flying high in the sky.*

D8-23. un-**suit**-a-ble: A KTM 125cc motocross bike is **unsuitable** for Chase because it is too big for him to ride. He can ride a KTM 65cc because it is suitable for him.

Group D9 Wise Owl Polysyllables

D9-1. **toad**-stool: A **toadstool** is a *mushroom that is believed to be inedible or poisonous.* They are called toadstools, but toads don't really sit on them!

D9-2. **freight**-er: A **freighter** is *a ship for carrying cargo in bulk.* Oil **freighters** cross the ocean carrying enormous amounts of oil to fuel our cars and factories.

D9-3. **roar**-ing: Have your heard of Aslan the Lion in the Chronicles of Narnia. You could hear him **roaring** for a long distance. He was a wise and kind Lion.

D9-4. **sleigh**-ing: Santa Clause is said to go **sleighing** every Christmas evening. A sleigh is a sled drawn by horses or reindeer to carry people. **Sleighing** is *to ride on a sleigh.*

D9-5. **toa**-ster: Wilma got a new **toaster** for her birthday. A **toaster** is *an electrical device for making toast.* Some folk like their toast dark and some like it light.

D9-6. eigh-**teen**: Julie was **eighteen** years old when she decided she wanted to learn to play the classical guitar. She concentrated on Renaissance Lute Music.

D9-7. un-ap-**proa**-cha-ble: A person who is approachable is friendly and easy to talk to. A person who is **unapproachable** is *not friendly or easy to talk to.* It is almost impossible to get close to a person who is **unapproachable**. Un- is a prefix for *not*.

D9-8. **weight**-less: Astronauts in outer space are **weightless**. They have no *weight* to hold them down, so they just float around in the spacecraft.

D9-9. **neigh**-bor-ly: Russell was very **neighborly**. He knew all his neighbors and was always friendly and helpful.

D9-10. **mo**-tor-boat: There are lots of **motorboats** on the Ohio River. **Motorboat** races are always exciting. A **motorboat** is just *a boat with a motor to make it move.* Mr. Whitlock of Rising Sun, Indiana, made a really fast motorboat that set a record that has never been broken.

D9-11. **fudge**: Katie likes lots of hot chocolate **fudge** on her vanilla ice cream.

D9-12. **rail**-road-ing: Gary checks the railroad tracks to makes sure they are safe for the trains. He has been involved in **railroading** for over thirty years.

D9-13. **dodg**-er: A **dodger** is *someone who tries to get out of an unpleasant situation by a cunning trick*. Morgan tried to dodge (avoid) her responsibility to rake the leaves by saying she had a sore on her right hand.

D9-14. **quick**-ly: Because she woke up late, Susie got ready for work **quickly**. She got ready *real fast*. **Quickly** is an adverb because it ends in –ly and modifies verbs.

D9-16. **quack**-ing: It is fun to visit the duck pond and listen to all the ducks **quacking**. Ducks make good pets. Some kids confuse *quick* and *quack* because they look alike.

D9-17. **lodge**: Jean and Rodger were going to **lodge** at the Hunter's **Lodge** all weekend. They were going to *stay* at the hunter's *cabin*.

D9-18. **square**-ly: The teacher placed the blame **squarely** on Rebecca's shoulders for not doing her homework. She looked her in the eye and told her it was all her fault.

D9-19. mis-**judge**: The teacher **misjudged** the new student when she said that he could not do the work. She had made a *wrong judgment* concerning his ability.

D9-20. **li**-quid: **Liquid** is one of the three states of matter. The others are solid and gas. Jan poured the green **liquid** into a glass.

D9-21. **crawl**-ing: Babies craw on their hands and knees. Doctors have discovered that **crawling** is an important part of their physical and mental development. All babies need to crawl a lot in order to be healthy and smart.

D9-22. **con**-quest: One of Mr. Potter's favorite books is titled the <u>History of the **Conquest** of Peru</u> by William H. Prescott. It tells how a small band of brave Spanish soldiers conquered the huge Inca Nation.

D9-23. **qual**-i-ty: The Martin Guitar Company makes high **quality** acoustic guitars. Doc Watson was a famous bluegrass guitar player who played Martin Guitars.

D9-24. e-**quip**-ment: Mountain climbers' success depends on having the right kind of **equipment**. They have special shoes, tents, oxygen supplies, warm clothing, and food that provide a lot of energy for the strenuous climb. They are well equipped to climb.

D9-25. **quar**-ter-mas-ter: A **quartermaster** is a *military officer responsible for housing, food, clothing, and other supplies.* The **quartermaster** is one of the most important men in the army because he keeps everybody housed, fed, and clothed.

D9-26. un-**law**-ful: **Unlawful** means *not lawful.* It is **unlawful** to drive a motorcycle down the halls of our school. Do they ride motorcycles in your school?

Group E Symbol-to-Sound Relationships

g ou ow ch ea oo ey ei
…ed augh ough ear sion ie pn

Group E1 Wise Owl Polysyllables

E1-1. **games**-man-ship: **Gamesmanship** is *the art of winning games by using special tactics to gain a psychological advantage*. Junior made a lot of noise to distract his brother when they played horseshoes so he would miss the ringer. His **gamesmanship** strategy was distraction.

E1-2. **mess**-age: King Arthur sent a **message** to the Knights of the Round Table to come and help him fight off the evil invaders. He sent them all a *written note*.

E1-3. **gun**-boat: The Union Army used big **gunboats** on the rivers to attack Rebel strongholds. They had powerful cannons mounted on the boats.

E1-4. **ran**-ger: Cindy the friendly Park **Ranger** showed the campers where to set up their tents. She knew everything about the forest and how to camp safely.

E1-5. **dog**-gie: My little Chihuahua **doggie** used to chase rabbits down the rabbit hole.

E1-6: sug-**gest**-ing: "Are you **suggesting** that we fly to Indiana instead of drive the family car?" "Yes," said Dad, "that is my suggestion." "Great!" exclaimed Mom and the kids, "Let's take a fast jet." "Okay," said Dad.

E1-7. **gift**-ed-ness: Ruby played the violin like Yehudi Menuhin. Both had **giftedness** for playing advanced violin pieces at a tender, young age. They had a *natural ability*.

E1-8: **gen**-ius: Albert Einstein was a true **genius**. He had *exceptional intellectual and creative powers*. His discovery of the Theory of Relativity was one of the greatest discoveries of modern times.

E1-9: for-**get**-ting: **Forgetting** is *a failure to remember*. Don forgot where he had laid his pocketbook. He *couldn't remember* where he put it until his wife discovered that it had fallen behind the dresser.

E1-10. stra-**te**-gic: The school has been involved in **strategic** planning. They are making *long range plans* to see how the school can grow and improve.

E1-11. **big**-gest: The Saturn V Rocket is the **biggest** rocket ever built. It is *bigger than any other* rocket ever built. NASA is currently working on a bigger rocket to get to Mars.

E1-12. ge-**og**-ra-phy: Mr. Lowe studied **geography** in college. He studied the *physical features of the earth and its activities*.

E1-13. **gadg**-et: An electric pencil sharpener is a handy **gadget** to have in a classroom. A **gadget** is *a small mechanical device or tool*.

E1-14. **pas**-sen-ger: Jill was a **passenger** on the new **passenger** train. **Passengers** are *people who ride on public or private vehicles that someone else is driving.*

E1-15. **tri**-an-gle: Billy drew a big **triangle** on the wall in his bedroom. It was a very nice **triangle** with *three sides and three acute angles.* He got in big trouble with his mom.

E1-16. ter-mi-**nol**-o-gy: **Terminology** refers to *words that are peculiar to a subject of study.* In the study of physics, we use words like atoms, protons, gravity, force, reaction, light, heat, and other such words.

E1-17. **gar**-den-er: Sam Gangee was Frodo Baggins' **gardener** in the Lord of the Rings. Do you have a garden? A *gardener takes care of the plants in a garden.*

E1-18. **lon**-gi-tude: Sailors use their knowledge of **longitude** and latitude to determine the location of their ship on the globe. Lines of **longitude** go from north to south.

E1-19. a-**gain**: It was great to communicate with my old high school friends *again.* I had to meet with them on the Internet since they live too far away to visit personally.

E1-20. tau-to-**log**-i-cal: **Tautological** is a big word, but it just means *to say the same thing again with a different word.* The words *orthography* and *spelling* mean the same thing. They are **tautological** words.

E1-21. to-**geth**-er-ness: Mr. Potter and his son often camped in a little dome tent. They experienced a lot of **togetherness** camping together in that little tent.

E1-22. how-**ev**-er: Henry never gave up trying to learn Morse Code, **however** difficult it may have seemed. He was going to learn it *regardless of how* difficult it was.

Group E2 Wise Owl Polysyllables

E2-1. **sig**-na-ture: Mr. Potter has a book with his dad's **signature** in the front. His dad wrote his *name in cursive* on the first page of the book to indicate that it was his book.

E2-2. **now**-a-days: **Nowadays** everybody sends emails instead of writing letters by hand. It is faster but less personal. **Nowadays** means *the present time and not the past time*.

E2-3. **rec**-og-nize: It is important for you to learn to **recognize** words quickly and accurately if you are going to enjoy reading. To **recognize** is *to identify something you learned before*. Literally it means *to know again*.

E2-4: **ma**-ga-zine: One of Mr. Williams' favorite **magazines** is Acoustic Guitar. It is filled with information on great guitars and great guitar players.

E2-5: **voy**-age: The **Voyage** of Dr. Doolittle is a great story about a doctor who could talk to animals. Mr. Potter read all the Dr. Doolittle books when he was a little boy.

E2-6: or-ga-**nize**: If you **organize** your books by subjects, you will be able to find a particular book faster. Libraries have all their fiction books organized by author.

E2-7: in-au-gu-**ra**-tion: President Lincoln's address at his Second **Inauguration** is very famous. An **inauguration** is *the formal admission of someone to office*. In Abraham Lincoln's case, it was his Second **Inauguration** into the office of the President of The United States of America.

E2-8. **au**-to-graph: An **autograph** is another word for a *signature*. It comes from two Greek words: auto (self) and graph (write). Baseball players often **autograph** baseballs for their fans. They write their names on the balls.

E2-9. **sau**-sage: Susie had **sausage** for lunch. It is made of *seasoned pork, beef, or other meat encased in a skin*.

E2-10. **wreck**-age: The underwater archeological team found the **wreckage** of an Ancient Roman ship at the bottom of the Mediterranean Sea. **Wreckage** is *the remains of any thing that has been damaged or destroyed*.

E2-11. gra-**phol**-o-gy: **Graphology** is *the study of a person's handwriting to infer a person's character*. Your handwriting can reveal a lot concerning your personality. Some people think that good handwriting instruction can help improve your personality.

E2-12. **lodg**-ing: Jim was **lodging** with his cousins who lived high up in the mountains. He was *staying* with them.

E2-13. prop-a-**gan**-da: Many tyrants throughout history have used **propaganda** to control their citizens. They *mislead people with false information to promote their political cause.*

E2-14. **brow**-nies: My Mom makes delicious **brownies**. **Brownies** are *small squares of chocolate cake with nuts.*

E2-15. lit-i-**ga**-tion: **Litigation** looks like a hard word, but it just means the *process of taking legal action.* Jimmy went to his lawyer to start **litigation** to get his neighbor to quit dumping trash in his backyard.

E2-16. **owl**-ish : Here is a word you don't see everyday. Owls are supposed to be wise creatures. An **owlish** person is *someone who is very wise like an owl.* You are learning to read big words with WISE OWL Polysyllables.

E2-17. **ca**-gey: **Cagey** means *secretive.* Susie was very **cagey** about her plans for the weekend.

E2-18. **clown**-ing: The boys were **clowning** around on the monkey bars. They were having fun *fooling around.*

E2-19. **large**-ness: The onlookers marveled at the **largeness** of the aircraft carrier. It was *really big.*

E2-20. **flower**-less: The plant in our front yard is **flowerless** right now because the little rabbit ate the flower. The plant has *no flowers* right now.

E2-21. gem-**ol**-o-gist: Mary wanted to be a **gemologist**. A **gemologist** is *a person who studies precious gems*.

E2-22. **horse**-pow-er: James Watts, the inventor of a practical steam engine, adopted the term **horsepower** to express the *power* of his steam engine.

Group E3 Wise Owl Polysyllables

E3-1. **ger**-my: **Germy** is the *adjective form of germ*. They cleaned the cafeteria with disinfectant because it was **germy**. **Germs** *are little living creatures that can make you sick*.

E3-2. **know**-ing-ly: Kim asked, "Did he **knowingly** trip the little girl?" Ruth replied, "No, he did not know she was running when he happened to stick out his foot and accidentally tripped her. He apologized anyway."

E3-3. **blow**-ing: Sonny Terry was a great blues harmonica player. He was always **blowing** into his harmonica and making great music.

E3-4. **re**-course: Mrs. Hiskes has no **recourse** but to teach phonics to everybody with reading problems who comes to her for tutoring. It is the best *source of help to turn to in this difficult situation*.

E3-5. **slow**-ly: Julie walked **slowly** to the chalkboard when Mrs. McKinley asked her to work the hard algebra problem. She *took her time* walking to the chalkboard.

E3-6. **show**-man-ship: Donald showed real **showmanship** when he stood on his head for five minutes. It as **a great performance** everybody enjoyed.

E3-7. **court**-ly: In <u>The Princess Bride</u>, Wesley showed **courtly** love to Princess Buttercup. There has never been another love like it in all the history of the world.

E3-8. **soul**-ful-ness: Sonny Terry's blues harmonica playing was full of **soulfulness**. He put his whole soul into playing and touched everybody's hearts with his soulful music.

E3-9. **flow**-ing: I guess you know that you will never see water **flowing** uphill in a stream. The **flowing** stream *just keeps moving along* forever and ever down stream.

E3-10. dis-**course**: Mr. Blumenfeld gave a historic **discourse** on the advantage of cursive handwriting. He delievered *a formal discussion* of all the many advantages of cursive.

E3-11. **own**-er-ship: The **ownership** of fountain pens is something you don't see much these day. **Ownership** is *the act, state, or right of possessing something.*

E3-12. four-**teen**: Mary was **fourteen** (14) years old yesterday. **Fourteen** is a *cardinal number* equivalent to the product of seven and two: 7 x 2 = 14.

E3-13. **glow**-worm: A **glowworm** is *a little beetle that glows in the dark, especially the larva like wingless female.* **Glowworms** are also called *fireflies* and *lightening bugs.*

E3-14. **you**: I included this little word just to teach the phonogram ou with the /o͞o/ sound in **you**. **You** should know how to spell *you*!

E3-15. **grow**-ing-ly: Here's a word you will not see very often. It is an adverb meaning *more and more*. The Black Forest became **growingly** dense and entangling as we penetrated into the dark interior.

E3-16. **youth**-ful-ness: Youthful is an adjective as in "youthful boy." Add the suffix –ness, and you get a noun as in the sentence, "**Youthfulness** depends more on your state of mind than your age."

E3-17. **spar**-row: Did you know that **sparrows** are not native to America. They are *little brown and gray birds* that came over from the Old World.

E3-18. **wound**-ed: The brave soldier was **wounded** in the famous Battle of the Bulge during WW II. He was shot in the arm, but completely recovered.

E3-19. **el**-bow-ing: Mrs. Harper does not allow any **elbowing** in her lunch line. No student is allowed *to use his or her elbows to crowd to the front of the line.*

E3-20. **your**-self: To modernize Shakespeare,
   This above all: be true to **yourself**,
   And it must follow, as night follows day,
   You cannot be false to anyone else.

E3-21. **yel**-low: **Yellow** is a primary color. I included it here to teach the phonogram *ow* with the /ō/ sound. Marcia wore a lovely **yellow** ribbon in her hair today.

E3-22. a-**cous**-tics: Musicians are very interested in **acoustics**. **Acoustics** has to do with *sounds*. Acoustic Guitarists depend on the **acoustics** of their guitar, instead of electric amplifiers, to make beautiful musical sounds.

Group E4 Wise Owl Polysyllables

E4-1. **ar**-row-heads: Mr. Dorrell used to find Indian **arrowheads** when he plowed his fields. The Indians shaped flint rocks to make sharp arrowheads for hunting.

E4-2. **touch**-down: The Mighty Warriors made a winning **touchdown** at the end of last Thursday's football game. In football a **touchdown** is *a six-point score*.

E4-3. **pil**-low-case: Sheila changes the **pillowcases** on her children's beds every week. The kids' **pillowcases** have pictures of bunny rabbits on them.

E4-4. **cous**-in: It is fun to have our **cousins** come over to play. They like to play a game of baseball after dinner. A **cousin** is *a child of one's uncle or aunt*.

E4-5. **fel**-low-ship: J. R. Tolkein's Fellowship of the Ring is one of the most famous adventure novels of all time. It is the first volume of three in The Lord of the Rings.

E4-6. **coun**-try-side: In The Hobbit by J. R. Tolkein, we read about the beautiful **countryside** in the Shire where the Hobbits lived a quite life before the coming of The Ring. The Magic Ring led Bilbo Baggins into all kinds of thrilling adventures.

E4-7. **round**-a-bout: **Roundabout** is *traveling somewhere taking the longer route rather than the shorter direct route.* Terry and Kim took the long **roundabout** route to our house so they could take in all the beautiful sights.

E4-8. ri-**dic**-u-lous: Harvey told a **ridiculous** story about a clown riding a mountain bike to the top of Mount Everest. It even had snow tires! The story was *absurdly impossible.*

E4-9. **ground**-ed: Casey's airplane was **grounded** for a couple of days because of bad weather. He was *not allowed to fly* because the weather was too dangerous for flight.

E4-10. su-per-**sti**-tious: Mickey was very **superstitious**. He never walked under a ladder because he said it might bring him bad luck, but one time he walked under a ladder and nothing bad happened so he isn't **superstitious** any more.

E4-11. our-**selves**: We decided to treat **ourselves** to a juicy watermelon that a vender was selling along the roadside. **Ourselves** is a *reflexive pronoun.* Did you know that?

E4-12. **child**-ish-ness: **Childishness** is *a noun used for something that is childish.* Adults should put away **childishness** and act like responsible adults. It is childish to cry every time that we do not get our way.

E4-13. **hour**-glass: Christopher Columbus used an **hourglass** to keep track of time. An **hourglass** *uses the passing of sand to measure one hour's time.*

E4-14. **chick**-en-pox: Mr. Wilbur had the **chickenpox** when he was a little boy. It is *a contagious illness that makes you itch a lot*. It can leave scars on your body.

E4-15. foun-**da**-tion: A house is no stronger than its **foundation**. The **foundation** is *the lowest load-bearing part of a building*. Usually it is underground.

E4-16. **church**-go-er: Ronald and Donald are **churchgoers**. They *go to church* to learn about the Bible and worship God with songs and prayers.

E4-17. **hou**-ses: Why do you think some kids read "horses" when they see the word "**houses**?" They need to learn *Mr. Potter's Secret of Reading*: "Look at all the letters the right way and no guessing."

E4-18. **hair**-piece: Some girls like *to add some detached hair to augment their natural hair*. They attach the **hairpiece** to the hair they already have. They think it is cute.

E4-19. **mount**-ed: When we moved to our new house we **mounted** pretty pictures on all the walls. The prettiest is one that Mrs. Rita Burrows made me of a beautiful country scene in Indiana, where I grew up. It is *fastened* to the wall in my office.

E4-20. **tea**-ches: Mr. Potter **teaches** Spanish, reading, and cursive handwriting at his private school. He *gives the students lessons* in all those subjects.

E4-21. a-**bout**: I was thinking **about** all the fun my brother Ron and I used to have on our dad's dairy farm in Indiana. We worked hard, but we also got to go swimming everyday!

E4-22. **chap**-ter. Mr. Potter's favorite **chapter** in The Fellowship of the Rings is **Chapter** 10, where Sam refuses to leave Frodo. Sam is faithful to Frodo, his beloved master.

Group E5 Wise Owl Polysyllables

E5-1. **moun**-tain-side: Jesus preached his famous Sermon on the Mount on a **mountainside** in Galilee. He preached it on the *side of a mountain.*

E5-2. **sand**-wich-es: Tuna **sandwiches** are very good for your health. Take two slices of bread and put some delicious tuna between them and you have a tuna sandwich.

E5-3. out-**stand**-ing: Rodger did an **outstanding** job playing violin for the bluegrass concert at Farmers Retreat in Indiana. His playing *stood out as the best.*

E5-4. **hand**-ker-chief: A **handkerchief** is a *square piece of cotton cloth for blowing or wiping your nose.* It is good to have one with you at all times in case you have to blow your nose.

E5-5. an-**nounce**-ments: It is important to pay attention to **announcements** at school so you won't miss out on anything. An **announcement** is *a public statement.*

E5-6. **cho**-co-late: Mr. Potter has a **chocolate** party every year for fourth grade, when he finishes reading <u>Charlie and the Chocolate Factory</u> in Spanish to his Spanish class.

E5-7. **school**-room: When Mr. Potter's dad went to **school** the school only had one teacher and one schoolroom for eight grades. Mrs. Pearl Monroe taught all the subjects.

E5-8. **heav**-i-ness: The suffix –ness turns an adjective into a noun. Heavy becomes **heaviness** when you add –ness. The **heaviness** of the couch was very great so we hired a mover to move it. Think of other words ending in –ness.

E5-9. **Christ**-like-ness: Susie had **Christlikeness** because she always treated people fairly and with love *like Christ did* when he lived on this earth.

E5-10. **bear**-a-ble: It was a very hot day in the tropics, but the breeze made the heat **bearable**. We were *able to endure* the heat thanks to the cool breeze.

E5-11. **chord**-ing: Good guitar players know all about **chording** to make their music harmonious. They know how *to arrange the notes in the chords* to sound good.

E5-12. **break**-fast-ing: We were **breakfasting** on the back porch since it was nice outside. We *ate our breakfast* outside in the open air.

E5-13. **sched**-ul-ing: It is good to use a calendar when **scheduling**. **Scheduling** is *making a plan to do something at a certain time*. Mr. Potter schedules his tutoring appointments so he can tutor as many students as possible each day.

E5-14. **weath**-er: The **weather** is perfect for the mountain bike race. There is a clear blue sky and a gentle breeze.

E5-15. **stom**-ach-ache: Austin had a **stomachache** after the chocolate party. I told him not to eat too much chocolate. Now his *stomach hurts*.

E5-16. **pleas**-ant-ness: Add –ness to the adjective pleasant and you get the noun **pleasantness**, which means *enjoyment*. I enjoyed the **pleasantness** of the cool day.

E5-17. **tooth**-ache: Rodney had a bad **toothache**, but Dr. Meek was able to repair the tooth and stop the pain. A **toothache** is *an ache or pain in a person's tooth*.

E5-18. al-**read**-y: Harvey told his mom that he had **already** done all his homework. He did it on time so he could go out and play.

E5-19. Chris-ti-**an**-i-ty: **Christianity** is *the religion based on the person and teaching of Jesus of Nazareth*. You can learn all about it in the books of the New Testament.

E5-20. **feath**-er-y: Sylvia had **feathery** blond hair. It was as *soft and light as a bird's feather*.

E5-21. **char**-ac-ter: Balsar Brent was a leading **character** in the great adventure book, <u>Bears of Blue River</u> by Charles Major. A **character** is *a person in a story.*

E5-22. **heav**-en-ly: Grandma's saltwater taffy is **heavenly**. It is *very delicious and wonderful* to eat.

Group E6 Wise Owl Polysyllables

E6-1. ma-**chine**: Notice that the ch in **machine** has the /sh/ sound, not /ch/ This is because it comes from the French language. Other words are: *brochure, chagrin, charlatan, mustache, parachute, Cheryl, Michelle, Chicago*, and *Michigan.*

E6-2. **par**-a-chute: A **parachute** is *a large piece of cloth that is used to allow a person or object to fall safely from a great height.* André-jaques Garnerin made the first parachute descent on October 22, 1797, when he jumped 3,200 feet from a hydrogen filled balloon.

E6-3. **each**: The little word **each** is included here in order to teach the phonogram ch that makes the /ch/ sound at the end of a word. Each word is important, however little.

E6-4. **read**-er-ship: Every author hopes to have a big **readership**. They hope that *lots of people read their books.*

E6-5. **dear**-ly: June **dearly** loved the beautiful German fountain pen her mother brought her from Germany. She *really* liked the way it wrote smoothly on the paper.

E6-6. **clean**-ing: **Cleaning** the house was not one of Betty's favorite chores. She would rather read a good book.

E6-7. **broad**-leaf: The leaves of a walnut tree are **broadleaves**. Its leaves are *very broad*.

E6-8. **deal**-er-ship: We bought our last car from Honest Bill's Car **Dealership**. Honest Bill promises to give everybody a good deal on a used car.

E6-9. **ear**-phone: It seems like everybody these days is walking around with **earphones** in their ears listening to music. At least they are not bothering other people with their loud music.

E6-10. **mean**-ing-ful: Mr. Potter uses **meaningful** sentences to teach the meanings of polysyllables. Dr. George González taught him how many years ago.

E6-11. **dream**-er: Mr. Potter is a **dreamer**. He dreams of teaching all boys and girls to read well with his WISE OWL Polysylables.

E6-12. im-**mea**-sur-a-ble: **Immeasurable** good can be done by dedicating one's life to teaching others how to read and write expressively. Won't you join me in this endeavor that is *beyond measure* in the good it can do? Together we can do **immeasurable** good.

E6-13. **right**-ly: Richard quipped, "They **rightly** do inherit heaven's graces," when Rodger told him about how kind his sister was to everybody. Richard was quoting a sonnet by William Shakespeare. I hope you read Shakespeare's sonnets.

E6-14. **bright**-ness: Here is another word with the noun building suffix –ness. I love to gaze into the sky at night and contemplate the **brightness** of the moon and stars.

E6-15. **might**-i-ly: America's Founding Fathers worked **mightily** to found a Republic that would insure the citizens' liberty to pursue the noble ends of life.

E6-16. **knight**-hood: Ivanhoe is a famous novel by Sir Walter Scott about **knighthood** and chivalry. A man *became a knight* when he received **knighthood** from the king.

E6-17. **flight**-less: An ostrich is a **flightless** bird. It is *a bird that cannot fly*.

E6-18. **fight**-er: The Spitfire was one of the fastest **fighter** planes of the Second World War. The British designed, built and flew the Spitfire, which successfully fought off the German bombers in the Battle for Brittan.

E6-19. **sun**-light: Everybody needs **sunlight** to produce vitamin D, which is necessary for good health. The *light of the sun* is necessary for good health.

E6-20. **mid**-night: In the blackness of the **midnight**,
The wind is hushed,
And the bedroom window
Bears a tiny light.

E6-21. de-**light**-ful-ly: **Delightfully** the fairies danced
In the pale moonlight.
They danced and danced
All through the night.

E6-22. to-**night**. Did you know the letter *o* in *tonight* is a schwa sound (tə nī′). The schwa is like a short-ŭ. There is a good movie **tonight**.

Group E7 Wise Owl Polysyllables

E7-1. **eas**-i-ly: June found she could **easily** open the hardest jar lid with a special jar opener. It was *easy* to open the jars once she got the jar opener. The suffix –ly makes adverbs.

E7-2. **flash**-light: We keep a **flashlight** with fresh batteries at all times in our classroom at school. In case of an electrical outage, we might need the *portable light*.

E7-3. **sea**-son-a-ble: Apples and oranges are **seasonable** fruits. They only grow during the summer season. They do not grow in the cold winter seasons.

E7-4. **zoo**-keep-er: Branden wants to be a **zookeeper**. He thinks it would be great fun *to take care of animals in the zoo*.

E7-5. **preach**-er: A good **preacher** will not put you to sleep when he tells a good Bible story. He knows his Bible well and can make the Bible stories exciting.

E7-6. dis-ap-**pear**-ing: The magician did a great **disappearing** act when he made a giant airplane disappear in thin air. He made the plane appear *to disappear* with an optical illusion.

E7-7. **food**-stuff: Some people think a doughnut is a good example of **foodstuff**. I prefer apples, grapes and bananas!

E7-8: **head**-band: A **headband** is *a band of cloth that can really help keep perspiration from running down in your eyes* during a long mountain bike race on a hot day.

E7-9. **fool**-ish-ness: It is sheer **foolishness** to let a ten year old drive a car in traffic. They *lack the good sense and judgment* at that young age to make good drivers.

E7-10. bal-**loon**-ist: Jeremy is a hot air **balloonist**. He *flies balloons as a sport or pastime.*

E7-11. **moon**-light: By the bright **moonlight**,
        I see the skinny fingers
        Of the trees caress the stars.

E7-12. **kang**-a-roo: A **kangaroo** *is a large plant-eating marsupial with a long powerful tail and strong hind limbs that enable it to travel by leaping.* Look up marsupial in a dictionary.

E7-13. **picked**: The -ed in **picked** makes the unvoiced /t/ sound because it follows an unvoiced consonant. Did you know that before you **picked** up this book?

E7-14. **look**-out: Mark served as a **lookout** for the Fifth Army during WW II. He was on the **lookout** for the enemy. He was *watching* for them.

E7-15. **hooked**: Mr. Potter is incurably **hooked** on dark chocolate, the darker the better. He thinks he should have some dark chocolate everyday. He *craves* it.

E7-16. **ba**-king: To bake is *to cook food by dry heat without direct exposure to a flame, usually in an oven or on a hot surface.* Jennifer is *baking* a delicious birthday cake for her boss.

E7-17. ad-**dress**-ing: The Parent Teacher Organization is **addressing** envelopes with information on the next fund raiser for the school. They are *writing addresses* on them.

E7-18. **foot**-lock-er: My dad had a **footlocker** at the end of his bed in his army barracks during Basic Training for the Army. It was a *small storage chest at the foot of his bed* where he stored his personal belongings.

E7-19. **rob**-ber-y: The Great Train **Robbery** was the first movie with narration. Before that movie, all movies were silent. **Robbery** is *the act of robbing.*

E7-20. **poor**-er: My dad used to say, "The rich get richer and the poor get **poorer**," referring to the fact that the rich have money to invest to make more money, and the poor don't. Jim is **poorer** than Susie because Jim has *less money and resources* than Susie.

E7-21. **wind**-shield: A hail storm broke the **windshield** in Kenny's car last Friday. It is called a **windshield** because it *shields (protects) the driver's face from the wind and debris*.

E7-22. **griev**-ance: Nancy filed a **grievance** with the judge when her neighbor built an ugly horse shed close to her house. She had a good reason for her *complaint*.

Group E8 Wise Owl Polysyllables

E8-1. **cen**-ter-piece: Betty put a beautiful **centerpiece** in the middle of her dining room table. A **centerpiece** is *a decoration put in the middle of a table*.

E8-2. a-**chieve**-ment: Landing a man on the Moon and returning him safely to Earth was one of mankind's greatest **achievements**. An **achievement** is *something done successfully that requires effort, courage, and skill*.

E8-3. mas-ter-**piece**: The Bach <u>Chaconne</u> is considered a **masterpiece** of Baroque Music. It is *a work of outstanding artistry*.

E8-4. **priest**-hood: Martin Luther is said to have rediscovered the **priesthood** of all believers. A priest is a person with a special relationship with God.

E8-5. **mis**-chie-vous: Roudy was a **mischievous** little boy. He was the Dennis the Menace of the second grade class. He was *always playing tricks* on the other students.

E8-6. dis-be-**lief**: Mr. Potter gazed in **disbelief** as he watched his son riding his new mountain bike on the dangerous trails at the Mountain Bike Park. He *couldn't believe it*. **Disbelief** is *when you don't believe something*.

E8-7. **pulled**: Uncle Bob's Potter's Allis-Chalmers WD Tractor **pulled** the heaviest sled at the tractor pulling contest at the Ohio County Fair one year. He won the pulling contest.

E8-8. **named**: Margaret **named** her dog, Rover. To name something is *to give it a name*.

E8-9. **good**-li-ness: **Goodliness** is the noun form of the adjective goodly. People who have **goodliness** are good people. We should all try to have **goodliness**.

E8-10. re-**turned**: I am sure you know that the prefix re- means "again." To return literally means, "*to turn again.*" Bob **returned** his library books on time.

E8-11. **foot**-ball: Everybody knows that a **football** is called a **football** because you kick it with your foot. Mr. Potter included it here to teach the oo that says /oo/.

E8-12. **lan**-ded: The United States Apollo 11 was the first manned mission *to land* on the moon. It landed on June 20, 1969. **Landed** is *the past tense of to land.*

E8-13. **good**-ness: David wrote in Psalms 23, "Surely **goodness** and mercy will follow me all the days of my life." **Goodness** is *the quality of being good.*

E8-14. de-**ci**-ded-ly: Mr. Potter is *decidedly* certain that good phonics is the key to high reading achievement. **Decidedly** means *undoubtedly* or *undeniably*. The –ly makes it an adverb.

E8-15. **neigh**-bor-hood: It is important to live in a good **neighborhood** where your neighbors are all good and friendly. Neighbors live together in a **neighborhood**.

E8-16. com-**ple**-ted: Jimmy **completed** his research paper on the history of quantum mechanics. He did the research, wrote the paper, and turned it in to Mr. Huron on time.

E8-17. **pock**-et-book: Julie has a new **pocketbook.** It is a cute **pocketbook** that is big enough to hold everything she needs to carry her everyday personal items.

E8-18. **thought**-ful-ness: **Thoughtfulness** is a wonderful thing. It refers to *the character of a person who is always thoughtful about others.* They care about the welfare of others.

E8-19. **bare**-foot-ed: It is fun to run **barefooted** in the soft grass. To run **barefooted** is to run *without shoes.* Some foot doctors think it is healthier to walk and run **barefooted**.

E8-20. through-**out**: Monica's house is clean **throughout**. Every room in her house is clean. **Throughout** means *all the way through*.

E8-21. **door**-mat: The **doormat** read, "Welcome." We included this word to teach the oo that says /ō/.

E8-22. **ought**: You **ought** to do your work. **Ought** is a common word with an Anglo-Saxon spelling. It is pronounced /aut/. It indicates one's *duty*.

Group E9 Wise Owl Polysyllables

E9-1. **floor**-ing: The oo in **flooring** is pronounced like a long o /ō/. *Door* and *floor* are two common words with the /ō/ pronunciation for the double-o. All the schoolrooms in our school have carpeting for **flooring**.

E9-2. **blood**-y: The oo in **bloody** is pronounced is the short-oo /oo/. Mark got a **bloody** nose when he fell out of the sycamore tree in the back yard.

E9-3. **flood**-ing: The oo in **flooding** is pronounced with the short-oo /oo/. The water was **flooding** into the basement after the terrible storm.

E9-4. **they**: Mr. Potter included the word, **they**, just to teach the phonogram ey that makes the /ā/ sound. He wants the phonics in his program to be complete.

E9-5. o-**bey**: It is good to **obey** your parents and teachers. You should *comply with their commands, directions, and requests*.

E9-6. **tur**-key: We had **turkey** for Thanksgiving Dinner. The ey in **turkey** makes the /ē/ sound. Notice the ey can make the /ā/ sound in *obey* or the /ē/ sound in **turkey**.

E9-7. **val**-ley: I went down to the **valley**
On a bright spring day
To play with my friends
In the merry month of May.

E9-8. **mon**-key: The ey in **monkey** rimes with key. Tarzan had a **monkey** for a pet. Can you yell like Tarzan?

E9-9. **hon**-ey-dew: You can buy **honeydew** melons from the roadside stand. The ew in **honeydew** makes the /o͞o/ sound as in *too*.

E9-10. **don**-key: A **donkey** is *an animal of the horse family with long ears and a braying call*. They make *good pack animals*. Bill was a famous **donkey** in the Lord of the Rings.

E9-11. at-**tor**-ney: An **attorney** is *a person who is appointed to act for another person in business or legal matters*, also called a *lawyer*. Perry Mason was a famous **attorney** in a television series of the same name.

E9-12. **bought**: Mr. Jones **bought** cans of sardines to take on his camping trip because they are easy to carry and do not need refrigeration. **Bought** is the *past tense of buy*.

E9-13. **dough**-y: Mindy did not cook the cookies long enough so they tasted **doughy**. They tasted almost like mushy, uncooked dough.

E9-14. su-per-**vi**-sion: Mr. Potter took a class in Administration and **Supervision** in college. It was an important class that taught him how to work well with other people. **Supervision** is *the action of supervising someone or something*.

E9-15. **brought**: The boys **brought** swimming trunks on vacation with them so they would be ready to go swimming in the hotel swimming pools. Ough has the /ô/ sound as in *bought* and *caught*.

E9-16. **fought**: Mr. Potter's dad **fought** with General Mark Clark's Fifth Army in North Africa and Italy during World War II. He **fought** to free the Italian people from their Nazi oppressors.

E9-17. al-**though**: **Although** means *in spite of*. **Although** Jacob failed his first spelling test, he got a 100% on the next one when his tutor helped him learn the words.

E9-18. e-**nough**: There are **enough** words in Mr. Potter's WISE OWL Polysyllable program to keep a student learning for a long time. Don't you agree?

E9-19. **earth**-en-ware: Daisy gave Mr. Potter an **earthenware** drinking jug and cup. They were made in Mexico from clay. They keep water cool on a hot day. Mr. Potter included this word to teach the sound of /ûr/ sound of *ear* in *earth*.

E9-20. learn-**ed**: Mr. Samuel L. Blumenfeld was a very learned man. He *learned a lot by studying a lot* about how to teach basic school subjects. Mr. Potter learned a lot from him. Mr. Blumenfeld wrote <u>The New Illiterates, Alpha-Phonics,</u> and several other great books.

E9-21. **heard**: Have you **heard** the news today? Notice that the phonogram *ear* can have the /ûr/ sound. **Heard** is the *past tense of hear.*

E9-22. **pearl**: Mrs. **Pearl** Monroe was Mr. Potter's first and second grade teacher. She was a beautiful lady, just like the beautiful **pearls** for which she was named.

Group E10 Wise Owl Polysyllables

E10-1. **their**: Although the word **their** is not a polysyllable, it is included here to teach the ei phonogram pronounced /ĕ/. **Their** is called a *possessive adjective.* **Their** house is big.

E10-2. **zeal**-ous: We should be **zealous** for good works. We should have an *active zeal (enthusiasm)* for doing good things for others. Margarita is **zealous** for teaching reading. She is *excited* about helping people read better with phonics.

E10-3. **re**-search: **Scientists** have done a lot of **research** into the best way to teach reading. They have *systematically investigated* many different methods for teaching reading. Mr. Potter followed the research and developed <u>WISE OWL Polysyllables</u> to be a scientifically validated method for helping YOU read better.

E10-4. **learned**: Kenny **learned** his arithmetic tables when he was very young. To learn is to *acquire knowledge by study*. He memorized all the tables by heart.

E10-5. un-**learned**: Un- is a prefix that means *not*. An **unlearned** person is one who has not acquired knowledge by study. It is *a person who is not well educated*.

E10-6. **ear**-ly: Benjamin Franklin used to say, "**Early** to bed, **early** to rise, makes a man healthy, wealthy, and wise. Modern doctors say Franklin gave good advice.

E10-7. **search**-light: **Searchlights** are *powerful outdoor electric lights with a concentrated beam that can be turned in any direction*. During WW II thousands of searchlights were used around industrial cities to search for incoming enemy aircraft.

E10-8. **cow**-boy: Gene was a **cowboy** who rode a paint horse to tend herds of cattle on the open range. He sometimes spent weeks on long cattle drives. **Cowboys** take care of cows.

E10-9. **daugh**-ter: Mr. Potter has three **daughters**. He loves them all, and they love him. Notice the augh in daughter. It has the /ô/ sound.

E10-10. **naugh**-ty: **Naughty** is another word with augh /ô/ in it. The **naughty** boy was *always causing trouble* at school.

E10-11. **caught**: The shortstop **caught** a high ball to win the game. It is another word with *augh* making the /ô/ sound. The phonogram *augh* is an Anglo-Saxon spelling.

E10-12. **pas**-sion-ate: I guess you know by now that Mr. Potter is **passionate** about teaching reading with phonics. He has *strong feelings* about the importance of teaching it.

E10-13. **mis**-sion-ar-y: Mr. Potter learned linguistics in a school to train **missionaries**. His teacher, Mr. Payden, was an expert in linguistics and language learning. The training was the key Mr. Potter used to learn Spanish and to become a better reading teacher.

E10-14. **ses**-sion: Mr. Potter had a weekly Spanish **session** with Mr. Zuniga, a native Spanish speaker from Mexico. A **session** is a *particular period devoted to a particular activity*.

E10-15. **man**-sion: Some Hollywood Stars live in **mansions**, which are *large impressive houses* that often cost millions of dollars.

E10-16. ex-**pres**-sion: Learning to write with **expression** comes from reading good literature and careful practice writing. **Expression** is *the process of making known one's thoughts and feelings*.

E10-17. con-**fes**-sion: **Confession** is one of the words Mr. Potter chose to teach the suffix –sion. It is pronounced as /zhon/ or /shon/. Here it is pronounced /sion/. Johnny **confessed** that he stole one cookie from the cookie jar. He *admitted* it, and said he was sorry and wouldn't do it again.

E10-18. **re**-a-lized: Junior **realized** that he had failed to do his math homework just in time to finish it on the way to school on the bus. He became *aware* of it just in time.

E10-19. **knowl**-edg-ea-ble: Werner Von Braun was very **knowledgeable** concerning the science of liquid rocket propulsion. He was *intelligent and well informed*. This word introduces the *ow* with the /ô/ sound as in *know*.

E10-20. **knowl**-edge: A good set of encyclopedias is a good source of **knowledge** about any subject. **Knowledge** is *what you know from study and experience*.

E10-21. ac-**knowl**-edge-ment: George received a letter of **acknowledgment** that he had been accepted to study at Indiana University. The *letter acknowledged* his admittance. It let him know he was accepted to be a student at the University.

E10-22. un-**known**: The New World was **unknown** until Christopher Columbus discovered it in 1492. **Unknown** means *not known*.

Group E11 Wise Owl Polysyllables

E11-1. **earth**-quake: The ground shakes and trembles during an **earthquake**. Strong earthquakes can cause a lot of damage to buildings and can be dangerous to people.

E11-2. a-**chiev**-ing: **Achieving** a high reading level requires learning eventually to read polysyllables. **Achieve** means *to reach or attain a desired level by effort*.

E11-3. **launch**-ing: The **launching** of the Sputnik on October 5, 1957, the first satellite to be launched into orbit, was a great technical triumph for Soviet scientists.

E11-4. **sand**-wich: The word **sandwich** was named after the Fourth Earl of Sandwich (1718-1792), an English nobleman, who is said to have eaten lots of sandwiches.

E11-5. chro-**nol**-o-gy: **Chronology** is *the arrangement of events or dates in the order of their occurrence.* Historians usually write in chronological order.

E11-6. **schwa**: **Schwa** is a modern symbol (ə) for the unstressed central vowel. Older dictionaries put a dot over the schwa sound: ȧ, ȯ, ė, and called them half-vowels.

E11-7. **chem**-i-stry: Be careful in **chemistry** class. **Chemistry** can be lots of fun, but mixing some chemicals can cause explosive reactions. Wear protective gear when working with potentially explosive or corrosive chemicals.

E11-8. **mus**-tache: Charlie Chaplin was a famous movie star who wore a **mustache**. A **mustache** is *a strip of hair left to grow above the upper lip.*

E11-9. **Mich**-i-gan: **Michigan** is a state in the northern US with borders touching four huge lakes. Many people in Michigan, who live along the lakes, own boats.

E11-10. ad-**dressed**: Be sure and put a return **address** on your letters. Your **address** is *where you live.*

E11-11. the-o-**log**-i-cal: A **theological** education is *an education about God and the things of God as He reveals them in nature and His word.* Jimmy received a **theological** education at Harvard University.

E11-12. **mag**-a-zine: Mr. Potter loves to read **magazines** about classical guitar music. He enjoys playing his beautiful music on his Takamine Electro-Acoustic Classical Guitar.

E11-13. **rec**-og-nize: I did not **recognize** the old house because the new owner had bricked over the wooden walls. To **recognize** is *to identify something we knew before.*

E11-14. **voy**-age: Mary and Henry went on a long **voyage** around the world in a sailboat. It was an exciting and dangerous *journey* with many perils.

E11-15. ar-**range**-ment: Mark sent his girlfriend a beautiful floral **arrangement** to let her know how much he loved her. The flowers were beautifully arranged in a rainbow of colors. They were *neatly put together in an organized way.*

Group E12 Wise Owl Polysyllables

E12-1. **con**-gress-man: The **congressman** from Texas *represented the interest of his constituents* in the Congress of the United States. He made sure the laws helped the people who voted for him.

E12-2. **le**-gal-ize: To **legalize** is *to make something previously illegal to be legal or permissible.*

E12-3. **ag**-o-nized: Julie **agonized** over whether to buy a blue dress or a red dress for the party. She *went through great mental pain and anguish worrying* about which to buy.

E12-4. non-cha-**lance**: Mr. Potter tried to demonstrate cool **nonchalance** when he announced that three of his students won a cursive writing contest. He tried *not to act excited*, but he was very happy and excited.

E12-5. pneu-**mat**-ic: A **pneumatic** socket wrench is a great help when taking off a nut that is rusted to a bolt. The *p* in **pneumatic** is silent. A **pneumatic** wrench is *one powered by compressed air or gas*. A **pneumatic** wrench is very powerful tool.

E12-6 pneu-**mon**-ia: The *p* in **pneumonia** is silent. It is a painful *inflammation of the lungs*. All words starting with *pn-* are from the Greek language. *Pn* is a two-letter Greek phonogram for /n/.

E12-7 pos-si-**bil**-i-ty: Mr. Potter thinks there is a good **possibility** that you now know all the big words in this book. He thinks there is a very *good chance* that you know them.

E12-8 gram-**ma**-ti-cal: Mr. Robert O'Neal teaches **grammatical** analysis. He teaches students how use grammar to parse and diagram English sentences. And he is good at it!

E12-9 lin-**guis**-tics: Mr. Payden taught Mr. Potter **Linguistics** for Learning Foreign Languages. **Linguistics** is *the scientific study of languages*.

E12-10. **pho**-no-gram: A **phonogram** is *a symbol for representing a speech sound*. PH is a Greek **phonogram** that represents the speech sound /f/.

E12-11. **graph**-eme: Linguists (people who study language) say that a **grapheme** is *the smallest contrastive unit in a writing system*. **Graphemes** can be one or more letters such as: *b, d, h, k, a, e, i, ch, sh, wh, th, ea, oy, oi*, etc.

E-12-12. **pho**-neme: /h/ /ē/ /t/ are the phonemes in the word *heat*. A **phoneme** is *a sound we can hear in a word that distinguishes it from another word*. The words *hot* and *pot* are distinguished by the **phonemes** /h/ in *hot*, and /p/ in *pot*.

E12-13. **spec**-tro-graph: Scientists use a **spectrograph** to analyze the elements in a substance. They heat up the substance and note what colors are emitted. The colors indicate the elements. Dr. Henry Draper invented the first spectrograph in 1876.

E12-14. my-**thol**-o-gy: A **mythology** is a *collection of myths* or *fictitious tales belonging to a particular religion or culture*. One well-known Greek myth tells how trouble came into the world when Pandora's curiosity caused her to open a mysterious box containing all kinds of evils that escaped into the world to cause trouble for everybody.

E12-15. or-**thog**-ra-phy: All schools need to teach English **orthography** to all the students. **Orthography** is a fancy name for *spelling*. Students who receive good spelling instruction become the best readers.

WISE OWL™ Polysyllabic Word Decoding Program

Word Statistics - 936 Words

Advancing Reading Skills for Advancing Readers

\multicolumn{5}{c	}{**Wise Owl Polysyllable Phonogram Groups**}
Group A	*Group B*	*Group C*	*Group D*	*Group E*
A1: 24	B1: 24	C1: 24	D1: 25	E1: 22
A2: 24	B2: 24	C2: 23	D2: 25	E2: 22
A3: 23	B3: 23	C3: 34	D3: 26	E3: 22
A4: 22	B4: 23	C4: 22	D4: 26	E4: 22
A5: 22	B5: 23	C5: 24	D5: 23	E5: 22
A6: 22	B6: 23	C6: 30	D6: 22	E6: 22
	B7: 20		D7: 22	E7: 22
	B8: 24		D8: 23	E8: 22
			D9: 26	E9: 22
				E10: 22
				E11: 15
				E12: 15
\multicolumn{5}{c	}{**Group Totals**}
Total: 137	Total: 184	Total: 147	Total: 218	Total: 250
\multicolumn{5}{c	}{**Cumulative Totals**}
137	321	468	686	936

The chart above can be used to record the student's progress by putting a check beside each Subgroup that has been completed.

Journal entries will serve as a record of the students' progress and will be one of their prize possessions for year to come.

WISE OWL Polysyllable Phonograms

Group A	Group B	Group C	Group D	Group E
1. a	22. or	26. ar	42. z	56. g
2. o	23. v	27. ng	43. aw	57. ou
3. s	24. p	28. sh	44. au	58. ow
4. m	25. wh	29. ay	45. kn	59. ch
5. d		30. ai	46. wr	60. ea
6. h		31. igh	47. oi	61. oo
7. b		32. k	48. oy	62. ey
8. th		33. ck	49. ph	63. ei
9. e		34. ur	50. oa	64. …ed
10. ee		35. ir	51. qu	66. augh
11. u		36. wor	52. ui	67. ough
12. t		37. j	53. eigh	68. ear
13. n		38. ew	54. dge	69. sion
14. r		39. ould	55. tion	70. ie
15. w		40. gn		71. pn
16. er		41. x		
17. f				
18. i				
19. y				
20. l				
21. c				
137 Words	**184 Words**	**147 Words**	**218 Words**	**250 Words**

WISE OWL™ Phonograms for Decoding Polysyllabic Words

Read the sounds between the slash marks: / /. The words to the right of the diacritical pronunciation symbol illustrate the sound.

WISE OWL Group A Phonograms

a	o	s	m
1. /ă/ cat	1. /ŏ/ pot	1. /s/ sis	/m/ mom
2. /ā/ cake	2. /ō/ go	2. /z/ is	
3. /ä/ father	3. /ŭ/ love		
4. /ȯ/ all	4. /o͞o/ to		

d	h	b	th
/d/ dad	/h/ hat	/b/ bib	1. /th/ the
			2. /th/ three

e	ee	u	t	n
1. /ĕ/ bed	/ē/ see	1. /ŭ/ cut	/t/ tot	/n/ noun
2. /ē/ me		2. /yo͞o/ cute		
		3. /o͞o/ music		
		4. /o͝o/ put		

r	w	er	f
/r/ roar	/w/ wag	1. /ûr/ her	/f/ fife
	(voiced)	2. /ār/ very	

i	y	l	c
1. /ĭ/ sit	1. /y/ yet	/l/ let	1. /k/ cat
2. /ī/ kite	2. /ĭ/ system		2. /s/ cent
3. /ē/ taxi	3. /ē/ really		"/s/ before e, i, or y"
	4. /ī/ fly		

WISE OWL Group B Phonograms

or	v	p	wh
/ôr/ b<u>or</u>n	/v/ <u>v</u>ase	/p/ <u>p</u>it	/hw/ <u>wh</u>en (unvoiced)

WISE OWL Group C Phonograms

ar	ng	sh	ay
/är/ f<u>ar</u>	/ng/ lu<u>ng</u>	/sh/ pu<u>sh</u> "/sh/ that begins and ends words	/ā/ d<u>ay</u> "two-letter /ā/ ends words

ai	igh	k	ck
/ā/ r<u>ai</u>n "two-letter 'ā/ that doesn't end words."	/ī/ h<u>igh</u> "three-letter /ī/."	/k/ <u>k</u>it	/k/ pa<u>ck</u> "two-letter /k/."

ur	ir	wor	j
/ûr/ f<u>ur</u>	/ûr/ f<u>ir</u>	/wûr/ <u>wor</u>d	/j/ <u>j</u>ar

ew	ould	gn	x
/eu/ bl<u>ew</u>	/o͞old/ sh<u>ould</u>	/n/ <u>gn</u>aw, si<u>gn</u> "two-letter /n/ that begins and ends words	/ks/ ta<u>x</u>

Skill Builder Group D Phonograms

z
/z/ zoo

aw
/au/ saw
"two-letter /au/"
that ends words."

au
/au/ haul
"two-letter /au/ that
doesn't end words

kn
/n/ knot
"two-letter /n/
that doesn't end
words.

wr
/r/ write
"/r/ that only

oi
/oi/ oil
" two-letter /oi/ that
doesn't end words."

oy
/oi/ toy
"two –letter /oi/
ends words."

ph
/f/ photo
Greek spelling

oa
/ō/ boat

qu
/kw/ quit

ui
/o͞o/ fruit
"two-letter /o͞o/."
that doesn't end words

eigh
/ā/ eight
"four-letter /ā/"

dge
/j/ edge
"three-letter /j/."

tion
/shun/ action

Skill Builder Group E Phonograms

g	ou	ow	ch
1. /g/ gag	1. /ou/ shout	1. /ou/ now	1. /ch/ church
2. /j/ gym	2. /ō/ pour	2. /ō/ row	2. /k/ school
/j/ before	3. /oō/ you	(vowel-consonant)	3. /sh/ chute
e, y, i or y.)	4. /ŭ/ young		
	(vowel-vowel)		

ea	oo	ey	ei
1. /ē/ beat	1. /oō/ too	1. /ē/ key	1. /ē/ receipt
2. /ĕ/ bread	2. /oŏ/ took	2. /ā/ they	2. /ā/ veil
3. /ā/ steak	3. /ō/ door	"/ē/ /ā/ that	
" /ē/ /ā/ that we	4. /ŭ/ flood	doesn't end words	
do use at the end			
of words."			

...ed	augh	ough
1. /ed/ wanted	/au/ caught	1. /au/ thought
2. /d/ opened		2. /ō/ dough
3. /t/ slipped		3. /ō/ though
		4. /ŭf/ rough

ear	sion	ie
1. /ēr/ ear	1. /zhŭn/ decision	1. /ē/ brief
2. /ûr/ early	2. /shŭn/ mission	2. /ī/ pie

pn
/n/ pneumatic

Introduction for Teachers

WISE OWL Polysyllable Decoding Program

WISE OWL stands for Word Identification Strategies of English: Orthographic Word Logic. Orthography is the study of spelling and how letters combine to represent sounds and form words. The title simply means a system for reading long words with phonics strategies. A polysyllable is a multisyllabic word.

History: The WISE OWL Polysyllable program was originally conceived as an approach to help older students who were struggling with reading. Mr. Frank Rogers of Tacoma, Washington, had a radically new idea for helping these students. He discovered that there were large classes of polysyllables (multisyllabic words) that consisted of phonics relationships (phonograms) that could be taught in a progressive order. Since the students have never read or memorized these longer words, they could be used to teach basic decoding skills. Noah Webster taught a similar class of polysyllables, which he appropriately designated, "Easy Polysyllables" in his 1824 *American Spelling Book*.

Personal Experience: I originally taught the program to second-grade bilingual students and first-grade monolingual English speaking students that had just finished mastering Mr. Rogers TATRAS reading program. I taught the program by just making up definitions and illustrative sentences for the kids on the spur of the moment. It later dawned on me that I could write definitions and sentences to go with the polysyllables. Having the sentences and definitions already written makes it easy for parents and teachers to help their children or students master the polysyllable decoding skills.

Syllables and Grade Levels: It is important to understand that reading levels are determined largely by sentence length (which assumes that long sentences are syntactically more advanced) and word length (which assumes that long words are semantically more advanced and difficult). Teaching younger children how to decode polysyllables allows them to increase their reading level dramatically by virtue of the part long words play in determining the reading levels.

Teaching Word Meanings: Most of the illustrative sentences and definitions are designed to be understandable to young children. It is excellent practice to have the children look up some of the words in a children's dictionary. All children should be taught how to use a dictionary to look up words, to determine pronunciation, to learn the spelling, and to grasp the meaning of words.

Syllable Division: The program does not specifically teach roots, prefixes, or suffixes, although they naturally occur in words of this length. I find that the students learn to decode these words and understand them without extensive labor in memorizing the morphemes themselves. This is the method of syllable division that Noah Webster used in all his spelling books and dictionaries. It is also the way syllables are divided in the respelling in modern dictionaries.

Phonogram Usage: No effort was made to restrict the words in the illustrative sentences and definitions to the phonograms being taught for each Phonogram Group. The students at this stage of reading development will know most of the words in the sentences and definitions. The teacher can pronounce and explain any words that the students may not know. I usually have the students read the sentences and definitions, but the teacher can read them to the student if that seems appropriate.

Instructions for Teachers: The program is very straightforward and easy to teach. Simply have the students sound out the polysyllable and read the short paragraph illustrating the meaning and usage of the word. The teacher can help with the sounding out and read the paragraph if necessary, as long as the student gains insight into the meaning and usage of the word. I have my students write the entry in spiral notebooks in cursive, although italic or manuscript would also serve the purpose. The notebooks become prize possessions for reference and review.

Students: The program is appropriate for students who have completed a good phonic reading program. I have taught it to students in first grade and up who are good readers. It can also be used with older students who desire to improve their reading skills.

Expectations: I have seen students in first grade improve from first grade level to as high as third through sixth grade levels on my 1987 *Riverside Informal Reading Inventory* upon completion of the program. Older students can make even higher gains.

ACKNOWLEDGMENTS

To Mr. Frank Rogers of Tacoma, Washington for his brilliant insights into the possibilities of classifying polysyllables according to restricted grapheme-to-sound correspondences, presented in a developmental sequence, as an aid in helping students to develop their phonics decoding skills and word identification fluency.

To Mr. Noah Webster for revealing to me the existence of easy polysyllables, when I was retyping his 1824 *American Spelling Book* in 2006.

To Dr. George González for teaching me how to teach English word meanings to Bilingual and ESL students using parallel sentences. This is the technique that I use in this program to teach the meaning of advanced English polysyllables to young English speaking students.

To experienced elementary teacher and reading researcher, Miss Geraldine Rodgers, for her research into the High Frequency Word Effect, which explains how young students can make a show of being able to read when their reading is in fact very defective. The High Frequency Word Effect refers to the fact that a very small number of words make up the majority of the words on any passage of written English. First-grade, second-grade, and third-grade teachers are often oblivious to the fact that their students are simply guessing the meaning of familiar words. When the vocabulary load outdistances the brain's ability to memorize words as objects, the students start falling behind.

To my wonderful second-grade bilingual students at the Murry Fly Elementary School in Odessa, TX during 2000-2001 & 2002-2003 school years and Mrs. Chavez' regular first-grade class. These were the first students that I taught the *WISE OWL Polysyllables*, demonstrating the fantastic power of the program to increase young children's grade level reading ability.

To my tutoring students at the Odessa Christian School in Odessa, TX, and my private tutoring students for helping me in the final phase of editing. They contributed significantly to the excellence of the program, as they worked with me through the program to improve their reading ability.

To Kathy González, a homeschool mother in Australia, for using my materials with her two young sons and for proofreading this manuscript. I could not have asked for a better proofreader. She was also helpful in proofreading my edition of Noah Webster's 1824 *American Spelling Book* and my edition of his 1908 *Elementary Spelling Book*. Mrs. González eight-year-old son, Daniel, drew the Wise Old Owl for the front cover and submitted the poem in the front of the book.

ABOUT THE AUTHOR

Mr. Donald L. Potter is an experienced teacher and serious student of the fine art and science of teaching reading.

At the time of publication of this document, Mr. Potter was in his tenth year teaching Spanish and Remedial Reading at the Odessa Christian School in Odessa TX. He also has a very active private tutoring practice during the summer vacation and after school.

He served as a public school teacher for twenty-one years for the Ector County Independent School District in Odessa, TX. He was an elementary bilingual teacher, Instructional Resource Teacher, dyslexia teacher, and secondary Spanish teacher. He also taught Amateur Radio Classes (NG5W) for seven years in the after school program.

His *Shortcut to Manuscript* and *Shortcut to Cursive* are very fine handwriting methods that are available for free from his website.

Among his published works for reading instruction available from Amazon or Barnes & Noble are: Florence Akin's 1913 *Word Mastery: Phonics for the First Three Grades*; Hazel Hazel Loring's 1980 *Reading Made Easy with Blend Phonics for First Grade with Blend Phonics Fluency Drills*; *Blend Phonics Lessons and Stories*; *Beyond Blend Phonics: English Morphology Made Simple*; *Playmates: A Primer, First Readers Anthology*; *Noah Webster's Spelling Book Method for Teaching Reading and Spelling*; *Psalms Reader: For Teaching Twenty-First Century Children to Read Fluently and Worship Their Creator*; *A Grammar of the Greek New Testament for Beginners*.

His website, www.donpotter.net, is a major source of the finest information on the best way to teach reading, writing, and spelling.

He is the founder of the *Blend Phonics Nationwide Educational Reform Campaign*.

Wise Owl Polysyllables was last edited on November 26, 2018.

Made in the USA
Coppell, TX
13 May 2020